a modo mio

Italian Cuisine

'my way'

contents

starters

-- *a fan of tomato & buffalo mozzarella*

-- *aubergine, mozzarella, tomato & parmesan timbales*

-- *bresaola with rocket & shavings of parmesan*

-- *bruschetta with artichoke pate`*

-- *bruschetta with aubergine, garlic & chilli flakes*

-- *bruschetta with fresh tomato & basil*

-- *bruschetta with garlic, oregano & extra virgin olive oil*

-- *bruschetta with gorgonzola & celery*

-- *bruschetta with roasted peppers & ricotta*

-- *chicken cocktail*

-- *chicken, roasted peppers & olive salad*

-- *giant green olives, stuffed & fried*

-- *pate` of pork with pistachio nuts & capers*

-- *roasted peppers & ricotta flans*

-- *salmon salad with olives, tomatoes & baby potatoes*

-- *tuna & borlotti beans salad*

-- *tuna & ricotta terrine with a lemon & oil dressing*

A FAN OF TOMATO & BUFFALO MOZZARELLA

ventaglio di pomodoro e mozzarella di buffala

4 large ripe tomatoes
4 buffalo mozzarellas about 150g each
20 basil leaves
4 tablespoons extra virgin olive oil
1 tablespoon balsamic vinegar
salt & freshly milled black pepper

SERVES 4

Put the tomato, stalk side down, on a
chopping board and cut slices into it without
cutting right down to the bottom.
Season with salt and pepper.
Cut the mozzarella into slices and place a
slice into each slit in the tomato.
Arrange the basil leaves on a plate, like a
flower and place the fan of tomato and
mozzarella on top.
Whisk together the oil and balsamic vinegar,
season with salt and pepper and drizzle over
each fan just before serving.

This dish is an attractive way of serving
caprese salad, which is sliced tomato
and mozzarella.

AUBERGINE, MOZZARELLA, TOMATO & PARMESAN TIMBALES

timbali di melanzane, mozzarella, pomodoro e parmigiano

2 aubergines
2 mozzarellas
100g grated parmesan cheese
400g tinned tomatoes, blended
1 onion, finely chopped
1 garlic clove, finely chopped.
4 basil leaves
6 tablespoons extra virgin olive oil
cooking oil
salt & freshly milled black pepper

SERVES 4

Trim and cut the aubergines into slices 2cm
thick and fry them, with just enough cooking
oil to cover the bottom of a pan, until golden
brown.
Make the tomato sauce; cook the garlic and
onion in a pan with the extra virgin olive oil
on a gentle heat until soft. Add the tomatoes,
basil, season with salt and pepper cook for
30 minutes.
Cut the mozzarella into slices.
Oil the insides of 4 metal cooking rings and
place them on a baking tray.
Start layering. Arrange the aubergine slices
on the bottom, spoon over the tomato sauce,
cover with mozzarella slices and sprinkle
on the parmesan cheese.
Continue to layer in this way finishing with
the tomato sauce and parmesan cheese.
Bake in the oven at 180C / gas mark 4 for
about 30 minutes, until golden brown.
Place the rings on warm serving plates,
run the blade of a knife around the inside
of the rings and lift them off.

BRESAOLA WITH ROCKET & SHAVINGS OF PARMESAN

bresaola con rucola e parmigiano

150g bresaola, thinly sliced
50g rocket leaves
100g shavings of parmesan cheese
4 tablespoons extra virgin olive oil
salt & freshly milled black pepper
juice of ½ lemon

SERVES 4

Arrange the slices of bresaola onto 4 plates,
slightly overlapping, to resemble the petals
of a flower.
Divide the rocket into 4 and pile on top of
the bresaola slices, in the centre.
Scatter the shavings of parmesan on top of
the rocket leaves.
Season with salt and pepper.
Whisk the oil with the lemon juice and just
before serving, drizzle over the top.

The flavours of the bresaola (cured beef),
together with rocket and parmesan are stunning.
This in larger quantities, is ideal in the summer
as a main dish.

BRUSCHETTA WITH ARTICHOKE PATE`

bruschetta con pate` di carciofi

8 slices of ciabatta bread
3 garlic cloves
200g of artichokes in oil
1 teaspoon chilli flakes
extra virgin olive oil
salt & freshly milled black pepper

SERVES 4

Drain the slices of artichokes and put them
into a food processor, add 1 garlic clove,
finely chopped, chilli flakes, salt, pepper
and blend.
Transfer to a bowl and pour in, a little at a
time, enough oil to make a smooth paste
and stir well.
Toast the slices of bread in the oven for 2
minutes each side. While still warm, rub
each slice with the garlic and spread the
artichoke pate` on top.

This pate` will keep for several days in an
air-tight container, in the fridge.

BRUSCHETTA WITH AUBERGINE, GARLIC & CHILLI FLAKES

bruschetta con melanzane, aglio e peperoncino

8 slices of ciabatta bread
1 large aubergine
3 cloves garlic
1 teaspoon chilli flakes
2 tablespoons extra virgin olive oil
salt & freshly milled black pepper

SERVES 4

Wash, trim and cut the aubergine into tiny dices. Put them in a pan with the oil, 1 garlic clove, finely chopped, chilli flakes, salt, pepper and cook for about 5 minutes till golden brown.
Toast the bread in the oven for 2 minutes each side. While still warm rub each slice with the garlic. Top with the aubergines.

This topping will keep for several days in an air-tight container in the fridge. Added to tomato sauce it makes a quick and tasty sauce for pasta.

BRUSCHETTA WITH FRESH TOMATO & BASIL

bruschetta con pomodoro fresco e basilico

8 slices of ciabatta bread
2 tomatoes
4 garlic cloves
6 basil leaves
3 tablespoons extra virgin olive oil
salt & freshly milled black pepper

SERVES 4

Put the tomatoes into a bowl of hot water
for 1 minute, peel them, remove the seeds,
and chop them into small dices.
Place them in a bowl with 2 garlic cloves,
cut in half and the basil leaves, roughly
chopped. Season with salt and pepper,
add the oil, mix well and leave to marinate
for ½ hour.
Toast the bread in the oven for 2 minutes
each side. While still warm rub each slice
with the garlic.
Top with the diced tomato, spoon over the
juices in the bowl and season with more
pepper.

Do not put the diced tomato on too far in
advance, as the bread will become soggy.

BRUSCHETTA WITH GARLIC, OREGANO & EXTRA VIRGIN OLIVE OIL

bruschetta con aglio, origano e olio extra vergine d'oliva

8 slices of ciabatta bread
3 garlic cloves
100ml extra virgin olive oil
2 tablespoons dried oregano
salt & freshly milled black pepper

SERVES 4

Pour the oil into a bowl, add the oregano,
one garlic clove, salt and pepper and mix
well.
Toast the slices of bread in the oven for 2
minutes each side.
While still warm, rub each one with the
garlic. Spread the oregano mixture
onto each slice.

These bruschettas are ideal to serve
with aperitifs.

BRUSCHETTA WITH GORGONZOLA & CELERY

bruschetta con gorgonzola e sedano

8 slices ciabatta bread
200g gorgonzola cheese
1 soft stem of green celery with leaves
1 soft stem of white celery
2 garlic cloves
freshly milled black pepper

SERVES 4

Cut the cheese into pieces and beat it in a
bowl until creamy. Clean, wash and chop
the celery stems and the leaves coarsely.
Mix the chopped celery with the gorgonzola
and season with the pepper.
Toast the bread slices in the oven for 2
minutes each side and while still warm, rub
each one with the garlic.
Spread the gorgonzola mixture on top and
serve while still warm.

This is a delicious starter, the gorgonzola when
spread on the warm bread melts slightly and is
best if eaten warm.

BRUSCHETTA WITH ROASTED PEPPERS & RICOTTA

bruschetta con peperoni arrostiti e ricotta

8 slices of ciabatta bread
2 garlic cloves
2 large roasted peppers
150g ricotta
1 tablespoon extra virgin olive oil
salt & freshly milled black pepper

SERVES 4

Slice the roasted peppers (ready roasted
ones are available) into thin strips.
Season with salt, pepper and add the oil.
Beat the ricotta until smooth and creamy,
season with salt and pepper.
Add the peppers to the ricotta and mix well.
Toast the slices of bread in the oven for 2
minutes each side and while warm, rub
each one with the garlic.
Top with the pepper and ricotta mixture.

This is a colourful and very tasty starter.
Red or yellow peppers can be used.

CHICKEN COCKTAIL

cocktail di pollo

500g boiled chicken
100g white celery
300ml mayonnaise
juice of ½ lemon
1 teaspoon Worcestershire sauce
1 teaspoon French mustard
2 tablespoons extra virgin olive oil
4 lettuce leaves
salt & freshly milled black pepper

SERVES 4

Cut the chicken into strips and put into a bowl.
Slice the celery finely and add it to the chicken. Season with salt and pepper, add the oil and mix well.
Put into another bowl, the mayonnaise, lemon juice, Worcestershire sauce, mustard and mix well. Add the chicken and celery, stir well, place in the fridge until serving time.
Wash, dry the lettuce leaves and arrange them in 4 sundae glasses.
Just before serving, divide the chicken cocktail into 4 portions and spoon each portion on top of the lettuce in the sundae glasses.

This dish is presented in the same way as prawn cocktail and is an alternative for people who do not eat fish.

CHICKEN, ROASTED PEPPERS & OLIVE SALAD

insalata di pollo con peperoni e olive

400g chicken breasts
1 carrot
1 onion
2 stalks celery
1 chicken stock cube
300g roasted peppers
200g silverskin onions
200g stuffed green olives, sliced
200g black olives, pitted & sliced
4 tablespoons extra virgin olive oil
salt & freshly milled black pepper
1 teaspoon chilli flakes

SERVES 4

Bring 1½ litres of water to the boil in a pan, add the stock cube, chicken breasts, carrot, onion, celery and cook for 1 hour.
Drain the chicken and leave to cool.
Slice the roasted peppers (ready roasted ones are available) and put them in a bowl with the green and black olives.
Take off the outer skin of the silverskin onions, cut them in half and add to the bowl.
Season with salt, pepper, chilli flakes, add the oil and mix well.
Cut the chicken into strips and add to the peppers and olives. Mix well.

The stunning colours of this dish makes it an attractive starter.
In larger quantities, it is ideal in the summer as a main dish.

GIANT GREEN OLIVES, STUFFED & FRIED

Olive ripiene

150g very lean pork
20 giant green olives, pitted
30g mortadella
50g parmesan cheese
2 eggs
200g breadcrumbs
100ml dry white wine
200ml meat stock
1 sprig rosemary
2 sage leaves
1 garlic clove
freshly milled black pepper
vegetable oil for frying

SERVES 4

Put the pork, garlic, rosemary, sage, wine
and stock in a saucepan, cover and cook on
a gentle heat for 30 minutes.
Drain the pork and when cool, put it into a
food processor with the mortadella, 1 egg,
parmesan and blend to a smooth mixture.
Season with pepper.
Carefully cut the olives along the open cavity
so they open out but are still in one piece.
Put an equal amount of the mixture into the
cavity of each one and press them closed.
Prepare two plates, one with the beaten egg
and the other with the breadcrumbs.
Coat each olive, first in the egg mixture then
in the breadcrumbs making sure they are
well covered.
If necessary repeat this procedure.
Put the vegetable oil in a frying pan and when
hot, fry the olives till golden brown.
Drain them with a slotted spoon and place on
kitchen paper to absorb any excess oil.
Serve warm.

PATE` OF PORK WITH PISTACHIO NUTS & CAPERS

pate` di maiale con pistacchi e caperi

500g very lean pork
150g butter
1 carrot chopped
1 onion chopped
2 celery stalks chopped
3 tablespoons olive oil
100ml dry white wine
100ml fresh single cream
1 tablespoon brandy
50g roasted pistachio nuts, chopped
30g capers, finely chopped
salt & freshly milled black pepper

SERVES 6-8

Put the pork into a saucepan with the oil,
carrot, onion, and celery.
Season with salt and pepper. Pour over the
wine, cover and cook on a low heat for 1½
hours, turning the meat occasionally.
Drain the meat and vegetables, put them in
a food processor and blend until smooth.
Work together the softened butter with the
cream and brandy and add this to the meat
mixture. Add 2 tablespoons of the juices
from the pan. Add the pistachios and capers.
Taste and if necessary, season with more
salt and pepper
Pour the mixture into a greased loaf tin
about 18cm x 9cm .
Cover with cling film and place in the fridge
for 4 hours. Remove from the fridge ½ hour
before serving.

This wonderful pate` is very delicate and also
is ideal for people who do not like liver.

ROASTED PEPPERS & RICOTTA FLANS

timbali di peperoni arrostiti e ricotta

1 jar roasted peppers (about 450g)
500g ricotta
3 egg yolks
2 tablespoons parsley, finely chopped
2 garlic cloves, finely chopped
2 tablespoons balsamic vinegar
4 tablespoons extra virgin olive oil
4 basil leaves
salt & freshly milled black pepper

SERVES 4

Mix the ricotta and egg yolks in a bowl, beat until smooth. Add half of the garlic, salt and pepper and beat again.
Cover the bottom part of 4 metal cooking rings with foil. Oil the sides and the foil and place them on a baking tray.
Cut the peppers to the size of the rings.
Place a piece of pepper in the bottom of each ring and spoon over the ricotta mixture.
Continue this procedure finishing with the ricotta mixture.
Cook in the oven at 180C / gas mark 4 for about 30 minutes until golden brown.
Place the rings onto serving plates, run a knife around the inside and lift them off.
Whisk together the oil, balsamic vinegar, parsley and the rest of the garlic and drizzle over the top of the flans, before serving.

These colourful and tasty flans make a wonderful starter and are ideal for vegetarians.

SALMON SALAD WITH OLIVES, TOMATOES, & BABY POTATOES

salmone con olive nere, pomodorini e patatine novelle

400g fresh salmon steaks
1 litre water
100ml dry white wine
½ onion
8 peppercorns
1 sprig rosemary
2 sage leaves
1 lemon
500g baby potatoes, boiled in their skins
200g black olives, pitted
300g cherry tomatoes
100ml extra virgin olive oil
1 lettuce
salt & freshly milled black pepper

SERVES 4

Put the water, wine, onion, rosemary, sage,
peppercorns, ½ lemon and salt in a pan and
bring to the boil. Cook for 10 minutes.
Add the salmon steaks and cook for a further
10 minutes. Drain them and leave to cool.
Break the salmon into bite-size pieces and
put them into a bowl.
Season with salt, pepper, add one tablespoon
of oil and mix well.
Put the potatoes, tomatoes, and olives into
separate bowls, season all with salt, pepper,
one tablespoon of oil and mix well.
Arrange the salmon, potatoes, tomatoes and
the olives on a serving dish decorated with
lettuce leaves.
Whisk the remaining oil with the juice of
½ lemon and drizzle this over the salad.

In larger quantities this salad is ideal, in the
summer, as a main dish. Rainbow trout can
also be used instead of the salmon.

TUNA & BORLOTTI BEANS SALAD

tonno e fagioli

2 x 200g tins tuna in olive oil
2 x 400g tins borlotti beans
½ onion
4 tablespoons extra virgin olive oil
1 tablespoon parsley, finely chopped
1 tablespoon lemon juice
1 lettuce
salt and freshly milled black pepper

SERVES 4

Slice the onion very finely and put it into a
bowl.
Drain the beans, add them to the onions,
season with salt and pepper and mix well.
Flake the tuna with a fork and add it to the
beans and onions.
Arrange the salad on a serving dish
decorated with lettuce leaves.
Whisk the oil with the lemon juice to a
smooth emulsion and drizzle this over the
salad.
Before serving, sprinkle over the chopped
parsley.

This hearty salad can be made in minutes
and in advance.

TUNA & RICOTTA TERRINE WITH A LEMON & OIL DRESSING

terrina di tonno e ricotta con salsina di limone e olio

2 x 200g tins tuna in olive oil
200g ricotta
3 large eggs, separated
salt & pepper
6 tablespoons extra virgin olive oil
juice of 1 lemon

SERVES 4-6

Heat the oven to 180 C / gas mark 4.
Drain the tuna from the oil and put it into a
food processor together with the ricotta, egg
yolks, salt and pepper, blend until smooth.
Whisk the egg whites until firm and fold in,
very gently, to the tuna mixture.
Pour into a greased loaf tin, 20cm x 11cm
and cook in the oven for about 40 minutes
till golden brown.
Remove the terrine from the dish and wrap
it in foil, this will stop it from drying.
Leave to cool.
When cold cut into slices and arrange them
on a serving plate.
Whisk together the oil, lemon juice, salt and
pepper to a smooth emulsion and pour this
over the slices.

This delicate terrine makes an ideal light
starter and is also ideal for picnics.

first courses

-- lasagne with aubergines

-- lasagne with pesto

-- minestrone

-- pappardelle with a creamy vegetable sauce

-- pasta & borlotti beans soup

-- pasta salad with roasted peppers & olives

-- pasta with a courgette, cream & white wine sauce

-- pasta with a creamy red & yellow pepper sauce

-- pasta with a mushroom, tomato & rosemary sauce

-- pasta with a prawn & asparagus sauce

-- pasta with a smoked salmon & white wine sauce

-- pasta with an aubergine, tomato & ricotta sauce

-- pasta with ragu` of prawns

-- potato gnocchi

-- risotto with asparagus, peas & courgettes

-- risotto with dried porcini mushrooms

-- risotto with leeks & mascarpone

-- risotto with smoked salmon & fresh spinach

-- spaghetti with a dried porcini mushroom sauce

-- spinach & herb crêpes with gorgonzola

-- bolognaise sauce

-- tomato sauce

LASAGNE WITH AUBERGINES

lasagne con melanzane

4 tablespoons extra virgin olive oil
400g tinned tomatoes, blended
1 garlic clove, finely chopped
1 onion, finely chopped
4 leaves fresh basil
2 large aubergines
250g lasagne sheets
400g mozzarella cheese
100g grated parmesan cheese
cooking oil
salt & freshly milled black pepper

SERVES 4

Cook the garlic and onion in the extra virgin olive oil on a gentle heat until soft.
Add the tomatoes, salt, pepper, basil and cook on a medium heat for 30 minutes.
Slice the aubergines lengthways and fry them with just enough cooking oil to cover the bottom of a frying pan, a few minutes each side, until golden brown.
Preheat the oven to 200C / gas mark 6.
Place the lasagne sheets in slightly salted boiling water for a few minutes, drain them and start layering.
Firstly, spread a little of the tomato sauce in the base of a rectangular oven-proof dish and lay the lasagne sheets on top then lightly cover them with the tomato sauce. Arrange the slices of aubergine on top, spoon over some tomato sauce, cover with the slices of mozzarella and sprinkle over the parmesan. Continue this procedure, finishing with a layer of tomato sauce and parmesan.
Cover with foil and bake in the oven for 30 minutes until bubbling and golden brown. Remove the foil and cook for a further 5 minutes.

LASAGNE WITH PESTO

lasagne al pesto

250g fresh lasagne sheets
150g parmesan cheese, grated
for the bechamel sauce
50g butter
50g plain flour
½ litre milk
salt & freshly milled black pepper
freshly grated nutmeg
for the pesto
100g fresh basil leaves
25g butter
4 tablespoons pine nuts
100g parmesan cheese, grated
4 garlic cloves, cut in half
extra virgin olive oil
salt & freshly milled black pepper

SERVES 4

Blend together the basil, pine nuts and the butter until smooth. Place in a bowl, season with salt, pepper and add the parmesan. Add enough oil to obtain a smooth paste. Spoon this into a jar, add the garlic cloves, leave to rest for 2 hours.
Melt the butter in a pan, add the flour, mix until smooth. Add the milk, stir and bring to the boil, whisking, until the sauce thickens. Season with salt, pepper and grated nutmeg. Put the lasagne sheets in salted, boiling water for 2 minutes.
Spread a little of the sauce on the bottom of a rectangular, greased baking dish and cover with a layer of the lasagne sheets. Put 2 tablespoons of pesto and 2 ladles of sauce on top, mix together and spread over evenly. Sprinkle over the parmesan. Repeat this process, finish with the sauce and parmesan. Cover with foil, bake in a pre-heated oven at 200C / gas mark 6 for 30 minutes till golden brown.

MINESTRONE

Minestrone

50g pancetta
4 tablespoons extra virgin olive oil
1 onion, finely chopped
2 stalks celery, thinly sliced
2 leeks, sliced
2 courgettes, diced
4 carrots, diced
2 large potatoes, diced
2 ripe tomatoes, peeled and chopped
200g butternut squash, diced
400g tinned borlotti beans
1 garlic clove, finely chopped
2 tablespoons parsley, finely chopped
1 tablespoon fresh basil, finely chopped
2 vegetable stock cubes
salt & freshly milled black pepper
120g arborio rice
2 tablespoons grated parmesan cheese

SERVES 4-6

Chop up the pancetta, fry it in a non-stick pan and discard the fat.
Put the oil, garlic and onion in a large pan and cook on a low heat until soft. Add the pancetta, celery, carrots, courgettes, leeks, potatoes, butternut squash and tomatoes.
Stir well and cook for a few minutes, add 2½ litres of warm water and stock cubes, cover and cook for 1½ hours on a medium heat.
Add the drained borlotti beans and cook for 10 minutes.
Add the rice and cook for 20 minutes.
Turn off the heat and sprinkle over the parsley and basil. Stir well.
Sprinkle with parmesan, season with pepper and a drizzle of extra virgin olive oil.

PAPPARDELLE WITH A CREAMY VEGETABLE SAUCE

pappardelle con sugo di verdure cremoso

500g fresh pasta - pappardelle
1 carrot
1 courgette
1 leek
½ red pepper
½ yellow pepper
½ green pepper
100g grated parmesan cheese
200g cream
100ml dry white wine
6 tablespoons extra virgin olive oil
salt & freshly milled black pepper

SERVES 4

Trim and wash the vegetables and cut them
all into thin strips (julienne).
Cook them with the oil, on a gentle heat, in
a pan big enough to hold the cooked pasta,
for about 10 minutes, until soft.
Season with salt, pepper, pour in the wine
and when it evaporates, reduce the heat and
add the cream. Stir well.
Add the cooked pasta to the vegetables and
stir well.
Turn up the heat, add the parmesan and mix
well together.
Before serving, season with lots of pepper.

Tagliatelle may be used for this dish instead
of the pappardelle.

PASTA & BORLOTTI BEANS SOUP

pasta e fagioli

2 x 400g cans borlotti beans
3 sprigs rosemary
2 garlic cloves, peeled
200g tinned tomatoes, blended
6 tablespoons extra virgin olive oil
1 tablespoon plain flour
salt and freshly milled black pepper
1 vegetable stock cube
200g short ribbed pasta
2 tablespoons grated parmesan cheese

SERVES 4

Put the olive oil, 2 sprigs of rosemary and
the garlic in a saucepan, cover and cook on
a low heat for 5 minutes.
Remove the rosemary, pour in the tomatoes,
mix well and stir in the flour.
Add the beans with their liquid, 1 litre of
water, stock cube, 1 sprig of rosemary,
cover and cook for 1 hour on a low heat.
Remove the garlic and rosemary from the
soup. Season with pepper, taste and if
necessary add more salt.
Add the pasta to the soup and cook until
'al dente'.
Sprinkle over the parmesan cheese.

This, once a poor man's meal, is now considered
a healthy dish and is served even in the top
restaurants in Venice.

PASTA SALAD WITH ROASTED PEPPERS, & OLIVES

pasta fredda con peperoni arrostiti e olive

300g pasta - farfalle
200g roasted red and yellow peppers
20 black olives, pitted
20 green olives, pitted
6 tablespoons extra virgin olive oil
4 garlic cloves, cut in half
6 leaves fresh basil, roughly chopped
1 teaspoon dried oregano
chilli flakes (optional)
salt and freshly milled black pepper

SERVES 4

Into a large bowl that will hold the pasta
when it is cooked, put the oil, oregano, basil,
salt, pepper and a pinch of chilli flakes.
Slice the peppers (ready roasted ones are
available) and add them to the oil mixture
together with the green and black olives.
Stir well, cover and leave to marinate for 2
hours.
Cook the pasta in boiling, salted water until
'al dente.' Drain and pass it quickly under
cold running water, this will stop the pasta
from cooking any further.
Drain well and add to the bowl. Stir well so
that the pasta is well coated.
Taste and if necessary season with more salt
and pepper.
Leave to cool in the fridge for a few hours.
Take out of the fridge 30 minutes before
serving.

It is best to use a good quality pasta for this
dish so that it doesn't lose its shape.

PASTA WITH A COURGETTE, CREAM & WHITE WINE SAUCE

pasta con zucchine e panna

350g pasta - farfalle or penne
500g courgettes, grated
2 shallots, finely chopped
1 garlic clove, finely chopped
1 tablespoon parsley, finely chopped
6 tablespoons extra virgin olive oil
100ml dry white wine
100ml single cream
2 tablespoons grated parmesan cheese
salt & freshly milled black pepper

SERVES 4

Put the oil, garlic, shallots in a pan, large
enough to hold the cooked pasta and cook on
a gentle heat until soft.
Add the courgettes to the pan, season with
salt and pepper, cook for 5 minutes and add
the parsley. Stir well.
Pour in the wine and cook for 2 minutes.
Stir in the cream, mix well and cook for 2
minutes.
Add the cooked pasta and stir well.
Before serving, sprinkle over the parmesan.

If possible use small dark green courgettes
as the larger ones are very watery when cooked.

PASTA WITH A CREAMY RED & YELLOW PEPPER SAUCE

pasta con sugo cremoso di peperoni gialli e rossi

350g pasta - penne or farfalle
2 red peppers
2 yellow peppers
6 tablespoons extra virgin olive oil
8 basil leaves
100ml fresh single cream
50g grated parmesan cheese
salt & freshly milled black pepper

SERVES 4

Wash and cut the peppers in half, take out
the white membrane, remove the seeds and
cut into pieces.
Put 4 tablespoons of the oil, into a pan large
enough to hold the cooked pasta and add
the peppers and basil.
Season with salt and pepper, cover and cook
on a gentle heat until the peppers are tender.
Pass all the contents in the pan to a food
processor and blend till smooth.
Return this to the pan, together with the rest
of the oil and cook for 2-3 minutes.
Stir in the cream and cook for 2-3 minutes.
Add the cooked pasta to the sauce and
stir well.
Before serving, sprinkle over the parmesan.

The combination of peppers, basil and cream
makes this pasta dish simply delicious.

PASTA WITH A MUSHROOM, TOMATO & ROSEMARY SAUCE

pasta con funghi, pomodoro e rosmarino

350g pasta - penne or rigatoni
300g button mushrooms, sliced
25g dried porcini mushrooms
400g tinned tomatoes, blended
2 garlic cloves, finely chopped
1 onion, finely chopped
100ml extra virgin olive oil
3 sprigs rosemary
100ml milk
salt and freshly milled black pepper
2 tablespoons grated parmesan cheese

SERVES 4

Put the dried porcini mushrooms into a bowl
of hot water and leave for 30 minutes.
Drain, rinse them under cold running water
and squeeze out any excess liquid. Chop up
into small pieces.
Put the oil, garlic, onion into a pan that will
hold the cooked pasta and cook on a gentle
heat until soft.
Add the tomatoes, season with salt, pepper
and cook for 30 minutes.
Add the mushrooms, porcini mushrooms and
rosemary to the tomato sauce, cover and
cook for 20 minutes.
Remove the rosemary from the pan, pour in
the milk, stir well and cook for 5 minutes.
Add the cooked pasta to the sauce and stir
well.
Before serving, sprinkle over the parmesan.

The milk added to the sauce gives it a creamy
consistency without using cream.

PASTA WITH A PRAWN & ASPARAGUS SAUCE

pasta con gamberi e asparagi

350g pasta - farfalle
1 bunch fresh asparagus
400g fresh prawns, peeled
1 large ripe tomato
6 tablespoons extra virgin olive oil
2 garlic cloves
100ml dry white wine
salt & freshly milled black pepper

SERVES 4

Wash the asparagus and trim off the woody
ends. Cut into diagonal pieces and blanch in
salted boiling water for 2 minutes.
Drain, rinse in cold water and set aside.
Put the oil into a pan that is big enough to
hold the cooked pasta and rub in the garlic.
Add the asparagus, season with salt and
pepper and cook for 2-3 minutes. Remove them
from the pan with a slotted spoon and keep
warm.
Place the prawns in the same pan, pour in
the wine and cook for 2-3 minutes.
Peel the tomato, remove the seeds and dice
the flesh into pea-size pieces. Add to the
prawns and cook for 1 minute.
Return the asparagus to the pan with the
prawns and tomato, cook for 1 minute and
stir well.
Add the cooked pasta and mix well.

Sometimes called the VIP pasta this is ideal for
dinner parties. It is delicious and refined, the
sauce can be prepared in the amount of time
it takes the pasta to cook.

PASTA WITH A SMOKED SALMON & WHITE WINE SAUCE

pasta al salmone affumicato

350g pasta - linguine or tagliolini
200g smoked salmon
25g butter
2 tablespoons extra virgin olive oil
100ml dry white wine
1 tablespoon plain flour
50ml milk
salt & freshly milled black pepper

SERVES 4

Cut the salmon into strips.
Put the butter and oil into a pan large
enough to hold the cooked pasta. When the
butter has melted, add the salmon, season
with salt, pepper and cook gently for 3
minutes.
Pour in the wine and cook for 5 minutes.
Remove the salmon from the pan with a
slotted spoon and keep warm.
Add the flour to the juices in the pan, stir
well and add the milk, cook for 2 minutes,
stirring, till the sauce is smooth and has
thickened slightly.
Return the salmon to the pan, stir well,
cook for 1 minute and add the cooked pasta.
Stir well and season with more black pepper.

Adding the flour and milk to the juices makes
this sauce creamy without using cream.

PASTA WITH AN AUBERGINE, TOMATO & RICOTTA SAUCE

pasta con melanzane, pomodoro e ricotta

350g pasta - rigatoni or penne
1 large aubergine
400g tinned tomatoes, blended
4 tablespoons extra virgin olive oil
1 garlic clove, finely chopped
½ onion, finely chopped
vegetable oil for frying
1 handful fresh basil leaves
100g ricotta
salt & freshly milled black pepper
2 tablespoons grated parmesan cheese

SERVES 4

Put the oil, garlic, onion into a pan large
enough to hold the cooked pasta and cook on
a low heat until the onion is soft.
Stir in the blended tomatoes and basil.
Season with salt and pepper, cover and cook
for 30 minutes.
Cut the aubergines into cubes, fry them with
just enough cooking oil to cover the bottom
of a non-stick frying pan, until golden brown.
Remove with a slotted spoon and drain them
on kitchen paper to absorb any excess oil.
Add them to the tomato sauce and cook for
5 minutes.
Stir in the sieved ricotta, mix well and cook
for a further 3 minutes.
Add the cooked pasta to the sauce, stir well
and cook for 1 minute.
Season with black pepper and sprinkle over
the parmesan.

For a more ' wicked' version of this dish,
add 100gr of mascarpone instead of the ricotta.

PASTA WITH RAGÙ OF PRAWNS

pasta con ragù di gambaretti

350g pasta - linguine or tagliolini
500g shelled prawns
4 tablespoons of extra virgin olive oil
1 small onion, finely chopped
1 carrot, finely chopped
1 stalk celery, finely chopped
1 garlic clove, finely chopped
400g tinned tomatoes, blended
100ml dry white wine
salt & freshly milled black pepper
1 tablespoon parsley, finely chopped

SERVES 4

In a pan large enough to hold the cooked
pasta, put the oil, onion, carrot, celery and
garlic. Season with salt and pepper, cover
and cook until very soft.
Chop the prawns finely and add to the pan,
mix well.
Pour in the wine and when it evaporates,
stir in the tomatoes.
Cover and cook for 30 minutes.
Add the cooked pasta, stir well and before
serving, sprinkle over the parsley.

Using chopped prawns instead of minced meat
makes this a very refined tasting pasta dish.

POTATO GNOCCHI

gnocchi di patate

1½ kg potatoes
300g plain flour
salt

SERVES 4

Boil the potatoes in their skins. Peel and
pass them through a potato mill and put
them into a large bowl.
While warm, add the sieved flour and salt.
Mix well with your hands and place onto a
floured worktop.
Divide the dough into pieces and roll each
one into sausage shapes about 2cm in
diameter. Cut into pieces about 2cm long.
Roll each piece onto a fork to shape.
Cook a few at a time in boiling salted water,
they are cooked as soon as they rise to the
top of the pan.
Put into a warm serving dish with, either
tomato or bolognaise sauce, stir gently to
avoid breaking them.
Sprinkle over the parmesan.

Gnocchi are best if eaten as soon as
they are made.

RISOTTO WITH ASPARAGUS, PEAS & COURGETTES

risotto con asparagi, piselli e zucchine

350g rice, arborio or carnaroli
1 bunch of asparagus
2 courgettes
100g peas, frozen
1 onion, finely chopped
100g butter
1½ litres chicken stock
100ml white wine
100g grated parmesan cheese

SERVES 4

Wash, trim the asparagus and cut into lengths of about 2cm, boil these in salted boiling water for 2-3 minutes, drain them and keep the tips apart.
Wash, trim the courgettes and slice them. Cook the peas in salted boiling water for 3 minutes and drain them.
Melt 50g of the butter in a heavy-based saucepan, add the onion and cook on a gentle heat until soft.
Add the asparagus, courgettes, peas, salt, pepper, cover and cook for 5 minutes.
Add the rice and stir until it is well coated.
Pour in the wine and when it evaporates start adding the stock, a ladle at a time, allowing each ladle to be absorbed by the rice before adding the next.
Stir well after each ladle of stock and cook until the rice is 'al dente'.
About 3 minutes before the rice is ready, add the asparagus tips.
Turn off the heat, add the remaining butter, stir well and leave to rest for a few minutes.
Before serving, sprinkle over the parmesan.

RISOTTO WITH DRIED PORCINI MUSHROOMS

risotto ai funghi porcini

350g rice, arborio or carnaroli
100g butter
1 onion, finely chopped
75g grated parmesan cheese
50g dried porcini mushrooms
1 teaspoon saffron powder
125ml dry white wine
125ml milk
1 litre meat or chicken stock
salt & freshly milled black pepper
2 tablespoons grated parmesan cheese

SERVES 4

Put the mushrooms into a bowl of hot
water and leave to soak for 30 minutes.
Drain them, reserving the water and rinse
under cold running water.
Squeeze out any excess liquid, dry them on
kitchen paper and chop up roughly.
Melt half of the butter in a heavy-based pan,
add the onion and cook on a low heat until
soft. Add the dried mushrooms, a ladle of
stock, season with salt and pepper and cook
on a gentle heat for 5 minutes.
Pass the soaking water of the mushrooms
through a fine sieve and add this to the pan.
Add the rice, cook for 2 minutes, stir well
until it is well coated and pour in the wine.
When it evaporates, start adding the stock, a
ladle at a time, allowing each ladle to be
absorbed by the rice before adding the next.
Ten minutes after the rice has been cooking,
add the saffron, milk and half of the
parmesan .When the rice is 'al dente', turn
off the heat, add the rest of the butter and
parmesan. Cover and leave to rest for a few
minutes before serving.

RISOTTO WITH LEEKS & MASCARPONE

risotto con porri e mascarpone

350g rice, arborio or carnaroli
100g butter
400g leeks, thinly sliced
100g mascarpone
100g grated parmesan cheese
1½ litres chicken stock
100ml dry white wine
salt & freshly milled black pepper

SERVES 4

Melt the butter in a heavy-based pan on a gentle heat and add the leeks.
Season with salt and pepper, cover and cook them on a gentle heat until very soft.
Add the rice, stir until it is well coated and pour in the wine.
When the wine evaporates, start adding the stock, a ladle at a time, allowing each ladle to be absorbed by the rice before adding the next. Continue cooking the risotto until the rice is 'al dente'.
Turn off the heat, stir in the mascarpone and leave to rest for a few minutes.
Before serving sprinkle over the parmesan.

For a lighter version of this risotto, crème fraîche can be used instead of mascarpone.

RISOTTO WITH SMOKED SALMON & FRESH SPINACH

risotto al salmone affumicato e spinaci freschi

350g rice, arborio or carnaroli
200g fresh spinach, chopped roughly
200g smoked salmon, chopped roughly
1 onion, finely chopped
80g butter
1½ litres chicken stock
100ml dry white wine
30g grated parmesan cheese
salt & freshly milled black pepper

SERVES 4

Put 50g of the butter in a heavy-based pan, add the onion and cook on a gentle heat until soft.
Stir in 150g of the salmon and cook for 2 minutes, add the spinach and cook for 2 minutes. Season with salt and pepper.
Add the rice and stir until it is well coated. Pour in the wine and when it evaporates, start adding the stock, a ladle at a time, allowing each ladle to be absorbed by the rice before adding the next. Continue to cook the risotto until the rice is 'al dente'.
3 minutes before the rice is ready, add the rest of the smoked salmon.
Turn off the heat, add the remaining butter, the parmesan and stir well.
Leave to rest for a few minutes before serving.

SPAGHETTI WITH A DRIED PORCINI MUSHROOM SAUCE

spaghetti con sugo ai funghi porcini secchi

400g spaghetti
400g tinned tomatoes, blended
4 tablespoons extra virgin olive oil
1 onion, finely chopped
40g dried porcini mushrooms
80g parma ham
50g grated parmesan cheese

SERVES 4

Soak the mushrooms for 30 minutes in a
bowl of hot water. Drain and rinse them
under cold running water, squeeze out any
excess liquid and chop them up roughly.
Cook the tomatoes, uncovered, for 30
minutes. Season with salt and pepper.
Put the oil and onion in a pan that will hold
the cooked spaghetti, cover and cook on a
gentle heat until very soft.
Chop up the parma ham finely and add to
the onion. Stir, cover and cook for 5 minutes.
Stir in the mushrooms to the onion and ham,
cover and cook for 5 minutes.
Add the tomatoes, stir well, cover and cook
for 5 minutes.
Add the cooked spaghetti to the sauce, mix
well. Season with pepper and sprinkle over
the parmesan.

SPINACH & HERB CRÊPES WITH GORGONZOLA

crespelle alle erbe ripene di gorgonzola

125g plain flour
3 eggs
250ml milk
150g butter
200g gorgonzola
100g fresh spinach
2 tablespoons parsley, finely chopped
2 tablespoons basil, finely chopped
pinch of grated nutmeg
4 sage leaves
2 tablespoons grated parmesan cheese
salt & freshly milled black pepper

SERVES 4

Wash the spinach, put it in boiling, salted
water for 1 minute. Drain and squeeze out
any excess liquid. Put it in a food processor,
blend with parsley, basil, salt and pepper.
Whisk the eggs with the salt in a bowl and,
while whisking, add the sieved flour. Pour
in the milk and keep mixing until smooth.
Leave to settle for 30 minutes then add the
spinach, herbs mixture and nutmeg.
Melt 50g of the butter and brush onto a
non-stick frying pan diameter 16-18cm.
Take the pan off the stove, pour in sufficient
batter to cover the bottom. Rotate the pan so
that the batter is evenly distributed, put the
pan back onto the stove and cook the crêpe,
until the edges start curling.
With a spatula, turn the crêpe over and
let the other side cook for a few seconds.
Prepare the other crêpes.
Spread each crêpe with gorgonzola, fold over
and arrange in a buttered oven-proof dish.
Melt the rest of the butter with sage leaves,
pour this over the crêpes, sprinkle with the
parmesan, cook in a pre-heated oven at
200C / gas mark 6 for 10 minutes till golden.

BOLOGNAISE SAUCE

salsa bolognese

4 tablespoons extra virgin olive oil
50g parma ham, finely chopped
1 onion, finely chopped
2 carrots, finely chopped
2 sticks celery, finely chopped
1 garlic clove, finely chopped
250g lean minced meat
50ml medium bodied red wine
400g tinned tomatoes, blended
400ml meat stock
4 basil leaves
2 cloves
1 teaspoon dried oregano
salt & freshly milled black pepper

SERVES 4

Put the oil into a saucepan, add the parma
ham and cook for 2-3 minutes. Add the onion,
carrots, celery and garlic, cover and cook on
a gentle heat until soft.
Season with salt and pepper, add the meat,
stir well and cook it until it changes colour.
Pour in the wine and when it evaporates,
add the tomatoes, basil, cloves, oregano and
stock.
Cover and cook on a very low heat for 1½
hours, stirring occasionally.

Minced beef, pork or turkey may be used for
this dish according to your taste.

TOMATO SAUCE

salsa di pomodoro

2 x 400g tinned tomatoes, blended
1 onion, finely chopped
2 garlic cloves, finely chopped
50ml extra virgin olive oil
4 basil leaves
salt & freshly milled black pepper

SERVES 6

Put the oil in a saucepan, add the onion and garlic, cook on a gentle heat until very soft. Do not allow to brown, if necessary add a very small quantity of water.
Add the tomatoes, and basil. Season with salt and pepper. Cover and cook for about 30 minutes, on a medium heat.
The sauce should have a dense consistency and should not be watery. If there is too much liquid, uncover and cook for a further 10 minutes.

This sauce will keep for about 1 week in an air-tight container in the fridge. It is useful to have ready as it is used in many of the recipes in this book.

meat dishes

-- *beef escalopes with a lemon sauce*

-- *beef escalopes with a marsala sauce*

-- *beef escalopes with a pizzaiola sauce*

-- *beef fillet steaks in a red wine sauce*

-- *beef parcels stuffed with parma ham & mozzarella*

-- *braised beef in Barolo wine*

-- *lettuce leaves stuffed with minced meat & ham*

-- *loin of pork, pot-roasted, with orange & wine sauce*

-- *meatballs with a tomato & sage sauce*

-- *meat loaf with a herb & wine sauce*

-- *pork chops with herbs & white wine*

-- *roast pork stuffed with herbs in a wine sauce*

-- *sausages & borlotti beans in a tomato & sage sauce*

-- *stuffed rolled steaks in a tomato sauce*

-- *t-bone steak with rocket & extra virgin olive oil*

BEEF ESCALOPES WITH A LEMON SAUCE

scaloppine di manzo al limone

8 thin beef escalopes about 100g each
3 tablespoons plain flour
50g butter
4 tablespoons extra virgin olive oil
4 tablespoons dry white wine
3 tablespoons lemon juice
salt & freshly milled black pepper
1 tablespoon parsley, finely chopped

SERVES 4

Put each escalope between two sheets of
cling film and pound until thin.
Season the flour with salt and pepper and
lightly coat the escalopes with this.
Melt the butter with the oil in a frying pan
and, when hot, fry the escalopes 2 minutes
each side, until lightly browned.
Remove from the pan and keep warm.
Add the lemon juice, wine and parsley to
the pan and cook for 2 minutes. Stir well.
Return the escalopes to the pan and cook
for 2 minutes, stir well so that they are
coated with the sauce.

This dish is best as soon as it is ready.
Ideal with creamed potatoes.

BEEF ESCALOPES WITH A MARSALA SAUCE

scaloppine di manzo al marsala

8 thin beef escalopes about 100g each
3 tablespoons plain flour
50g butter
4 tablespoons extra virgin olive oil
6 tablespoons marsala
salt & freshly milled black pepper

SERVES 4

Put each escalope between two sheets of
cling film and pound gently until very thin.
Season the flour with salt and pepper and
lightly coat the escalopes with this.
Melt the butter with the oil in a frying pan
and, when hot, fry the escalopes 2 minutes
each side, until they are lightly browned.
Remove them from the pan and keep warm.
Add the marsala to the pan, bring to the boil
and stir well.
Return the escalopes to the pan and cook for
2 minutes. Stir well so that they are coated
with the sauce.

This dish is best as soon as it is ready.
Ideal with creamed potatoes.

BEEF ESCALOPES WITH A PIZZAIOLA SAUCE

scaloppine di manzo alla pizzaiola

8 thin beef escalopes about 100g each
3 tablespoons plain flour
2 garlic cloves, finely chopped
2 tablespoons parsley, finely chopped
1 tablespoon capers, finely chopped
50g butter
4 tablespoons extra virgin olive oil
200g tomato sauce (recipe on page 54)
salt & freshly milled black pepper

SERVES 4

Put each escalope between two sheets of
cling film and pound gently until very thin.
Season the flour with salt and pepper and
lightly coat the escalopes with this.
Melt the butter with the oil in a frying pan,
and when hot, fry the escalopes 2 minutes
each side till lightly browned.
Remove from the pan and keep warm.
Put the garlic, parsley and capers in the pan,
season with salt and pepper and cook for 2
minutes. Pour in the tomato sauce, bring to
the boil and cook for 10 minutes.
Return the escalopes to the pan, cook for 2
minutes. Stir well so that they are coated
with the sauce.

This dish can be prepared in advance and is
ideal with polenta or creamed potatoes.

BEEF FILLET STEAKS IN A RED WINE SAUCE

filetto di manzo al vino rosso

4 beef fillet steaks about 150g each
400ml red wine
2 shallots
1 sprig of rosemary
2 sage leaves
2 garlic cloves
4 tablespoons extra virgin olive oil
2 tablespoons plain flour
25g butter
salt and freshly milled black pepper

SERVES 4

Put the wine, shallots, rosemary, sage and
garlic in a saucepan and bring to the boil.
Cook on a moderate heat till it reduces to
half the original volume.
Pass the sauce through a sieve and keep hot.
Lightly coat the steaks with the flour and
fry them in the oil until well browned on
each side.
Pour over the wine sauce, increase the heat
and cook for 10 minutes. Season with salt
and pepper.
Remove the steaks from the pan and arrange
on a warm serving dish.
Add the butter to the sauce, stir well, cook for
2 minutes and pour this over the steaks.

This dish is ideal for dinner parties.
The sauce can be prepared in advance.

BEEF PARCELS STUFFED WITH PARMA HAM & MOZZARELLA

scaloppine di manzo ripiene di prosciutto e mozzarella

8 thin beef escalopes about 100g each
80g mozzarella
60g parma ham
40g grated parmesan cheese
20g capers, chopped
16 black pitted olives, roughly chopped
1 tablespoon parsley, finely chopped
2 anchovy fillets, chopped
4 tablespoons extra virgin olive oil
100ml dry white wine
2 tablespoons plain flour
salt & freshly milled black pepper

SERVES 4

Put the escalopes between two sheets of
cling film and pound lightly.
Chop the mozzarella and parma ham very
finely, add the parmesan and mix well.
Divide this mixture into 8 parts and place
them onto the centre of each escalope. Fold
over and secure with a toothpick.
Lightly coat each 'parcel' with a little flour
and fry them with the oil till well browned.
Season with salt and pepper, remove from
the pan and keep warm.
In the same pan add the olives, capers,
anchovies and parsley, increase the heat
and cook for 2 minutes. Stir well.
Return the parcels to the pan, pour over the
wine, cover, and cook on a medium heat for
10 minutes.
Uncover and cook for a further 2 minutes.
Arrange on a warm serving dish and pour
over the sauce.

BRAISED BEEF IN BAROLO WINE

brasato al Barolo

1 kg topside in one piece
600ml Barolo or Barbera wine
60ml brandy
4 tablespoons extra virgin olive oil
2 carrots, chopped
2 onions, chopped
2 celery sticks, chopped
2 sprigs rosemary
1 tablespoon black peppercorns
½ cinnamon stick
3 cloves
1 stock cube
salt & freshly milled black pepper

SERVES 6

Put the beef in a large non-metal dish. Add the carrots, onions, celery, rosemary, cloves, cinnamon, peppercorns and pour over the wine.
Cover and leave to marinate for 24 hours, then drain the meat from the marinade and dry with kitchen paper.
Put the oil in a pan and when hot, add the meat and brown well on all sides. Season well with salt and pepper.
Pour over the brandy and cook for about 2-3 minutes till it evaporates.
Add all of the marinade, cover and cook on a low heat for 2½ hours stirring occasionally.
Drain the meat from the pan and keep warm.
Remove the rosemary and cinnamon then put the vegetables and liquid in a food processor and blend till smooth. Return this to the pan and cook for 3 minutes, stir well.
Slice the meat very thinly, arrange on a warm serving dish, and pour over the sauce.

LETTUCE LEAVES STUFFED WITH MINCED MEAT & HAM

foglie di lattuga ripene di carne e prosciutto

8 large lettuce leaves
250g lean minced beef
2 tablespoons extra virgin olive oil
100g cooked ham, finely chopped
100g grated parmesan cheese
50g butter
30g plain flour, sieved
300ml milk
pinch of grated nutmeg
200ml fresh single cream
salt & freshly milled black pepper

SERVES 4

Place the lettuce leaves in boiling water for
1 minute, drain and place them gently on
kitchen paper to dry.
Heat the oil in a pan, add the minced beef,
season with salt, pepper, cover and cook for
30 minutes.
Add the ham and 50g of the parmesan.
Melt the butter in a pan and stir in the flour.
Pour in the milk a little at a time, cook on a
low heat, stirring continuously, until the
sauce thickens. Season with salt, pepper and
nutmeg. Add this to the meat mixture, mix well
and leave to cool.
Divide the mixture into 8 portions and place
a portion in the centre of each lettuce leaf.
Gently fold the leaf over so that the mixture is
well covered and it resembles a little parcel.
Place the parcels in a greased ovenproof dish
with the folded part downwards.
Pour over the cream, sprinkle the parmesan
over evenly and cook in a preheated oven at
200C / gas mark 6 until golden brown.

LOIN OF PORK, POT-ROASTED, WITH AN ORANGE & WINE SAUCE

lonza di maiale all'arancia e vino bianco

800g loin of pork
2 oranges
4 tablespoons extra virgin olive oil
3 shallots, sliced
100ml dry white wine
½ teaspoon of tomato concentrate
1 bay leaf
a few fresh thyme leaves
400ml meat stock
salt and freshly milled black pepper

SERVES 4

Cut all the fat off the pork.
Put the oil in a pan and when hot, add the
pork, cook until well browned on all sides.
Add the sliced peel of 1 orange, cook for 3
minutes, add the shallots, and stir well.
Season with salt and pepper, add the
tomato concentrate, bay leaf and thyme.
Pour over the wine, cook for a few minutes
until the wine evaporates, add the juice of
the two oranges and two ladles of stock.
Cover the pan and cook on a low heat for
1½ hours, adding more stock if necessary.
Drain the pork and keep warm.
Remove the orange rind, put the shallots
and the juices into a food processor and
blend until smooth.
Return this to the pan, cook for 3 minutes.
Slice the pork very thinly, arrange on a
warm serving plate and pour over the sauce.

MEATBALLS WITH A TOMATO & SAGE SAUCE

polpettine al sugo di pomodoro e salvia

400g minced beef
2 slices bread, without crusts
2 eggs, lightly beaten
2 garlic cloves, finely chopped
2 tablespoons parsley, finely chopped
4 tablespoons plain flour
200ml milk
400g tomato sauce (recipe on page 54)
4 sage leaves
salt and freshly milled black pepper
cooking oil

SERVES 4

Soak the bread in 100ml of milk until soft.
Squeeze and put it into a bowl. Add the beef,
eggs, garlic and parsley. Season with salt
and pepper, and mix well.
Make the meatballs by taking pieces of the
mixture, about 1 tablespoon at a time, and
roll each one into a small ball.
Coat each one lightly with the flour and fry
in cooking oil until well browned.
Remove the meatballs with a slotted spoon
and drain them on kitchen paper to absorb
the excess oil.
Pour the tomato sauce into a pan, add the
sage, the rest of the milk and cook for 5
minutes. Taste and if necessary add more
salt and pepper.
Add the meatballs, cover and cook on a low
heat for 30 minutes. Uncover and cook for
a further 10 minutes, until the sauce has a
creamy consistency.

MEAT LOAF WITH A HERB & WINE SAUCE

polpettone alle erbe e vino bianco

800g minced beef
100g mortadella, finely chopped
2 slices bread, without crusts
100ml milk
4 garlic cloves,
2 tablespoons parsley, finely chopped
2 eggs, lightly beaten
2 sprigs rosemary
2 sage leaves
200ml dry white wine
6 tablespoons extra virgin olive oil
400ml meat stock
salt & freshly milled black pepper

SERVES 4

Soak the bread in the milk until soft, squeeze
and put it into a bowl. Add the meat, eggs,
mortadella, 2 garlic cloves and parsley.
Season with salt and pepper and mix well.
Put a sheet of foil on an ovenproof dish and
place the mixture on top. Shape it so that it
looks like a big sausage.
Cook in a pre-heated oven at 180C / gas mark
4 for 1 hour. Remove the meat loaf from the
oven and put it into a saucepan with the oil,
2 garlic cloves, rosemary, and sage.
Pour over the wine, 2 ladles of stock, cover
and cook on a gentle heat for 30 minutes,
adding more stock if necessary, so there is
enough sauce to pour over the meat loaf.
Remove the meat loaf from the pan, slice and
arrange on a warm serving dish.
Remove the herbs and pour the sauce over the
meat loaf slices.

PORK CHOPS WITH HERBS & WHITE WINE

braciole di maiale alle erbe vino bianco

4 large pork chops
4 tablespoons extra virgin olive oil
4 garlic cloves, halved
3 sprigs rosemary
4 sage leaves
100ml meat stock
200ml dry white wine
salt & freshly milled black pepper

SERVES 4

Trim the excess fat off the chops, fry them
in a pan with the oil until golden brown on
both sides. Season with salt and pepper.
Add the garlic, rosemary, sage, stock and
wine, cover and cook on a gentle heat for
about 1 hour.
They should be very tender and golden
brown.
Arrange the chops on a serving dish.
Remove the garlic, rosemary and sage from
the pan, and pour the sauce over the chops.

Pork chops cooked this way remain moist and
the meat just falls off the bone.

ROAST PORK STUFFED WITH HERBS IN A WINE SAUCE

arrosto di maiale farcito con erbe al vino bianco

1 kg loin of pork
4 garlic cloves
6 sprigs of rosemary
6 sage leaves
6 tablespoons extra virgin olive oil
200ml dry white wine
500ml stock made with 1 pork stock cube
4 tablespoons extra virgin olive oil
salt and freshly milled black pepper

SERVES 4

Put 2 garlic cloves, 4 sprigs of rosemary, 4
sage leaves into a processor and process
until very fine. Season with salt and pepper.
Remove all the fat on the pork.
With the point of a sharp knife make cuts all
over the joint and then insert the handle of a
wooden spoon into each cut to make it bigger.
Fill each of these cuts with the herb mixture.
Put the oil in a pan with 2 garlic cloves, 2
sprigs of rosemary, 2 sage leaves and when
hot, add the joint and cook it until well
browned on all sides.
Season with salt and pepper.
Pour over the wine and stock.
Cover and cook on a low heat for 1½ hours.
Drain the pork from the juices, slice very
thinly and arrange on a warm serving dish.
Remove the garlic, rosemary and sage from
the pan and pour the sauce over the pork.

SAUSAGES & BORLOTTI BEANS IN A TOMATO & SAGE SAUCE

salsiccia e fagioli con sugo di pomodoro e salvia

8 pure pork sausages
2 x 400g cans borlotti beans, drained
2 x 400g cans tinned tomatoes, blended
1 onion, finely chopped
2 garlic cloves, finely chopped
6 tablespoons extra virgin olive oil
100ml milk
6 sage leaves
salt and freshly milled black pepper

SERVES 4

Put the oil into a pan, add the onion, garlic and cook until soft. Add the tomatoes, salt pepper, cover and cook for 30 minutes on a medium heat.
If the sauce is too watery, uncover and cook for a further 10 minutes.
Add the borlotti beans, milk and sage leaves. Stir well, cover and cook for 10 minutes.
Cook the sausages in a non- stick frying pan until well browned all over. Add them to the beans and tomato sauce.
Cover and simmer gently for 40 minutes.
Serve with polenta or creamed potatoes.

This hearty dish is ideal for winter and best served with polenta. The sausages may be left whole or sliced after they have cooked and browned, before adding to the beans and tomato sauce.

STUFFED ROLLED STEAKS IN A TOMATO SAUCE

braciole di manzo ripiene al sugo di pomodoro

600g topside or rump steaks, thinly sliced
300g minced pork
100g mortadella, finely chopped
2 garlic cloves, finely chopped
2 tablespoons parsley, finely chopped
4 tablespoons extra virgin olive oil
400g tinned tomatoes, blended
100ml medium bodied red wine
4 large carrots, cut in half
1 onion
1 sprig rosemary
salt & freshly milled black pepper

SERVES 4

Place the steaks between two sheets of cling
film and pound gently.
Mix together the pork, mortadella, garlic,
and parsley. Season with salt and pepper.
Spread this mixture evenly onto each steak.
Roll up and tie with kitchen string.
In a pan, fry the rolled steaks in the oil until
they are well browned all over.
Season with salt and pepper, pour over the
wine and when it evaporates, add carrots
onion, rosemary and the tomatoes.
Cover and cook on a low heat for 1½ hours.

The steaks, cooked this way, almost melt in your
mouth. This dish can be prepared in advance.
Make it a complete meal by adding medium size
potatoes, cut in half about 15 minutes before
the meat is ready.

T-BONE STEAK WITH ROCKET & EXTRA VIRGIN OLIVE OIL

tagliata di manzo alla rucola

1 t-bone steak about 900g
4 cloves garlic, halved
2 sprigs rosemary
2 sage leaves
6 tablespoons extra virgin olive oil
50g rocket
salt & freshly milled black pepper

SERVES 6

Rub the steak with the garlic on both sides
and season with pepper. Leave to marinate
with the rosemary, sage and 2 tablespoons
of the oil for 2 hours.
Sprinkle some salt on a griddle pan and
when it is very hot, cook the steak on both
sides very quickly, to brown it and form
griddle marks.
Transfer to a greased ovenproof dish and cook
in a pre-heated oven at 200C / gas mark 6
for about 30 minutes.
The meat should be slightly pink inside.
For meat well done, cook for a further 10
minutes.
Cut the two parts of the meat away from the
bone, and slice them quite thinly, diagonally.
Arrange the slices on a serving dish, season
with salt, pepper and 2 tablespoons of oil.
Pile the rocket evenly on top of the meat and
drizzle over the rest of the oil.
Cover and leave to rest for 2 hours.

Ideal in the summer, this dish is very tasty
and very easy to prepare.

poultry dishes

-- *chicken breasts in a mushroom & mascarpone sauce*

-- *chicken cacciatora with polenta*

-- *chicken with peppers & olives*

-- *duck breast with a balsamic vinegar sauce*

-- *turkey breast filled with sun-dried tomatoes & olives*

-- *turkey breast slices in a tunny sauce*

-- *turkey breast with a courgette frittata filling*

-- *turkey parcels with cheese & ham in a wine sauce*

CHICKEN BREASTS IN A MUSHROOM & MASCARPONE SAUCE

petti di pollo con funghi e mascarpone

4 chicken breasts about 200g each
300g mushrooms, thinly sliced
30g dried porcini mushrooms
2 garlic cloves, finely chopped
2 tablespoons parsley, finely chopped
4 tablespoons extra virgin olive oil
200ml dry white wine
200g mascarpone
salt and freshly milled black pepper

SERVES 4

Soak the porcini mushrooms in warm water for 30 minutes, strain them in a sieve, keep the water, rinse them under cold running water. Squeeze out any excess water and chop them up roughly.
Put the oil, garlic, and parsley into a pan, add the button mushrooms and the porcini mushrooms. Season with salt and pepper, cover and cook for 15 minutes.
Take them out of the pan with a slotted spoon, so that the juices remain in the pan and keep warm.
Put the chicken breasts into the pan, and cook them until they are well browned.
Season with salt and pepper and pour over the wine.
Return the mushrooms to the pan, cover and cook, on a gentle heat, for 30 minutes.
Uncover, add the mascarpone, stir well and cook for a further 5 minutes.

CHICKEN CACCIATORA WITH POLENTA

pollo alla cacciatora con polenta

8 chicken thighs
3 carrots, finely chopped
4 stalks celery, finely chopped
2 onions, finely chopped
3 garlic cloves, finely chopped
2 tablespoons plain flour
4 tablespoons extra virgin olive oil
400g tinned tomatoes, blended
30g dried porcini mushrooms
200ml dry white wine
½ chicken stock cube
2 sprigs rosemary
salt & freshly milled black pepper
375g pre-cooked polenta

SERVES 4

Soak the porcini mushrooms in hot water for
30 minutes. Drain them, keep the water, and
rinse them under cold running water.
Squeeze out any excess liquid, dry on kitchen
paper and chop them up roughly.
Take the skin off the chicken thighs, season
with salt and pepper, lightly coat them with
the flour and fry them in the oil until golden
brown.
Cover them with the carrots, celery, onion
and garlic. Season with salt and pepper.
Pour over the wine, cover and cook for 15
minutes on a gentle heat. Add the tomatoes,
mushrooms, rosemary, stock, the water of
the mushrooms, cover and simmer gently for
1 hour, stirring occasionally. If the sauce is
too liquid, uncover and cook for a further
10 minutes. Remove the rosemary.
Arrange the thighs on a warm serving dish
and pour over the sauce. Cook the polenta for
5 minutes in 1½ litres of salted, boiling water.

CHICKEN WITH PEPPERS & OLIVES

pollo con peperoni e olive

8 chicken thighs
1 red pepper, thinly sliced
1 yellow pepper, thinly sliced
200g tinned tomatoes, blended
130g green olives, pitted
1 onion, thinly sliced
2 garlic cloves, thinly sliced
2 sprigs rosemary
200ml dry white wine
4 tablespoons extra virgin olive oil
2 tablespoons parsley, finely chopped
2 tablespoons plain flour
salt and freshly milled black pepper

SERVES 4

Remove the skin from the chicken thighs
and lightly coat them with the flour.
Heat the oil in a wide pan and fry the
thighs until golden brown.
Season with salt and pepper.
Add the onion, garlic, rosemary and wine,
cover and cook for 15 minutes. Stir well.
Cover the chicken with the peppers, olives
and tomatoes, cover and simmer gently for
1 hour, stirring occasionally.
If there is too much liquid, uncover, turn
up the heat and cook for a few minutes.
Arrange on a warm serving dish and
sprinkle over the parsley.

This colourful and tasty dish can be
prepared in advance. It is ideal with
polenta or creamed potatoes.

DUCK BREAST WITH A BALSAMIC VINEGAR SAUCE

petto di anatra all'aceto balsamico

4 duck breasts about 175g each
30g extra virgin olive oil
50g balsamic vinegar
20g butter
2 garlic cloves
2 sprigs rosemary
2 tablespoons plain flour
salt & freshly milled black pepper

for the sauce
100g extra virgin olive oil
90g balsamic vinegar
2 garlic cloves, finely chopped
6 basil leaves, finely chopped
1 teaspoon chilli flakes (optional)
salt & freshly milled black pepper

SERVES 4

Put the sauce ingredients into a bowl, mix
well and leave to marinate for 1 hour.
Take the skin off the duck breasts and coat
them lightly with the flour.
Put the oil, butter, garlic and rosemary into a
a pan, cook the breasts until well browned all
over and season with salt and pepper.
Pour over the balsamic vinegar, cover and
cook for 10 minutes.
Remove the duck breasts from the pan, cover
and keep warm. Leave to rest for 5 minutes.
Before serving, cut the breasts diagonally and
quite thinly then arrange them on a warm
serving dish and pour over the sauce.

TURKEY BREAST FILLED WITH SUN-DRIED TOMATOES & OLIVES

petto di tacchino ripieno di pomodori secchi ed olive

1 turkey breast about 800g
100g pancetta slices
8 giant green olives, pitted
8 sun-dried tomatoes, in oil
100ml dry white wine
4 sage leaves
2 garlic cloves
4 tablespoons extra virgin olive oil
400ml chicken stock
50g butter
salt & freshly milled black pepper

SERVES 4

*Cut the olives in half, drain the tomatoes
from the oil and cut them in half.
With a sharp knife make cuts in the turkey
breast and enlarge these cuts by inserting
into them the handle of a wooden spoon.
Put the olives and tomatoes into these cuts
alternatively.
Cover the breast with the pancetta slices and
tie up with kitchen string to keep it in shape.
In a saucepan put the oil, turkey breast, sage
leaves, garlic and stock.
Cover and cook on a low heat for 1½ hours.
Remove the breast from the pan, cut it into
thin slices and arrange them onto a warm
serving dish.
Remove the garlic and sage leaves, add the
butter to the juices and whisk until the sauce
starts to thicken slightly.
Pour the sauce over the slices of turkey.*

TURKEY BREAST SLICES IN A TUNNY SAUCE

tacchino tonnato

1 turkey breast about 800g
1 carrot
1 stalk of celery
1 onion
1 chicken stock cube
1 small tin of tuna in olive oil
1 small jar of light mayonnaise
2 tablespoons capers
2 tablespoons baby gherkins
juice of 1 lemon

SERVES 4

Put the carrot, celery, onion and stock
cube into a pan with 2 litres of water, and
bring to the boil.
Put in the turkey breast, reduce the heat and
cook for 1 hour. Take it out of the pan, cover
and leave to cool.
While it is cooking prepare the sauce, drain
the tuna from the oil and put it into a food
processor with capers, gherkins, 1 tablespoon
of the mayonnaise and blend until smooth.
Transfer this to a bowl, add the rest of the
mayonnaise and mix well.
Add the lemon juice and stir until the sauce
is smooth.
When the turkey breast is cold, slice thinly
and arrange on a serving dish.
Spoon the sauce over evenly making sure that
each slice is well coated. Decorate with a few
capers and baby gherkins.
Cover and place in the fridge for 2 hours.
This dish is best eaten the same day.

TURKEY BREAST WITH A COURGETTE FRITTATA FILLING

petto di tacchino ripieno di frittata di zucchine

1 turkey breast about 800g
2 eggs
2 courgettes, grated
3 garlic cloves
2 tablespoons parsley, finely chopped
8 tablespoons extra virgin olive oil
200ml dry white wine
400ml chicken stock
2 sprigs rosemary
4 sage leaves
salt & freshly milled black pepper

SERVES 4

Cut the turkey breast into one large slice.
Put this between two sheets of cling film,
gently pound it with a rolling pin until quite
thin and even.
In a small non-stick frying pan put 4 tablespoons of oil, 2 finely chopped garlic cloves,
parsley, cook for 2 minutes on a low heat
making sure the garlic does not brown.
Add the courgettes, salt, pepper, stir well
and cook for about 5 minutes until soft.
In a bowl, beat the eggs, add the courgettes,
salt and pepper. Return this mixture to the
frying pan and cook for 5 minutes on each
side until the frittata is golden brown.
Leave to cool. Put the frittata onto the turkey
breast and roll up together so it looks like a
big sausage. Tie with cooking string and put
it in a saucepan. Add the remaining oil, 1
whole garlic clove, sage, rosemary, wine and
stock and cook on a low heat for 1½ hours.
Take the breast out of the pan, remove the
string, cut it into quite thin slices and
arrange on a serving dish.
Remove the garlic, rosemary and sage from
the pan, and pour the sauce over the slices
of turkey.

TURKEY PARCELS WITH CHEESE & HAM IN A WINE SAUCE

tacchino con prosciutto e formaggio al vino bianco

8 slices of uncooked turkey about 100g each
8 slices of ham
8 slices of gruyère cheese
50g butter
4 sage leaves
100ml dry white wine
2 tablespoons plain flour
salt & freshly milled black pepper

SERVES 4

Put each slice of turkey between two sheets
of cling film and pound until thin.
On each slice of turkey place a slice of ham
and a slice of cheese, fold over, secure with
a toothpick. Lightly coat them with flour.
Melt the butter in a pan, add the sage and
turkey parcels, cook for a few minutes each
side until golden brown.
Pour over the wine, cover and cook on a low
heat for 30 minutes. Remove them from the
pan with a slotted spoon, and arrange them
on a warm serving dish.
Remove the toothpicks.
Pour the sauce over the turkey parcels.

This dish is best if eaten as soon as it is ready.

fish dishes

-- cod with a creamy onion, anchovy & parmesan sauce

-- fillets of sole in garlic, parsley, tomato & wine sauce

-- fillets of trout with king prawns & marsala

-- fillets of white fish in a courgette & wine sauce

-- fish kebabs

-- fish stew

-- mackerel fillets gratinated

-- salmon steaks with prawns & courgettes in a bag

-- sea bass baked with black olives & white wine

-- sea bream baked in a bag with tomatoes & olives

-- swordfish slices stuffed with olives & herbs

-- swordfish with olives & capers

-- trout in a red wine sauce

-- white fish fillets & pancetta with saffron & wine

COD WITH A CREAMY ONION, ANCHOVY & PARMESAN SAUCE

baccala alla vicentina

1 kg skinless fillet of cod
4 big onions, finely chopped
6 anchovy fillets, chopped
200ml olive oil
400ml milk
2 garlic cloves
150g grated parmesan cheese
50g flour
2 tablespoons chopped parsley
salt & freshly milled black pepper

SERVES 6

Preheat the oven to 180C / gas mark 4.
Gently cook the onions and garlic in 100ml
of oil until soft and transparent.
Stir in the parsley and anchovy fillets.
Season with salt and pepper and cook for a
further 5 minutes. Tip this into a greased
ovenproof dish.
Cut the fish into slices about 6cm wide.
Mix the flour and parmesan and roll the fish
in it, pressing the mixture on, so that it is
well covered. Arrange on top of the onions.
Mix the remaining oil with the milk and
pour this over the fish.
Bake for 40 minutes, till bubbling and golden.

This wonderful fish dish, typical of the Veneto
area is ideal in the winter.

FILLETS OF SOLE IN GARLIC, PARSLEY, TOMATO & WINE SAUCE

filetti di sogliola al pomodoro, aglio, prezzemolo e vino bianco

8 fillets of sole
2 cloves of garlic, finely chopped
2 tablespoons parsley, finely chopped
2 ripe tomatoes
1 teaspoon chilli flakes
100ml dry white wine
6 tablespoons extra virgin olive oil
salt & freshly milled black pepper

SERVES 4

Place the tomatoes in a bowl of boiling water
and leave for 10 seconds. Drain them and
peel off the skins.
Cut them in half, scoop out the seeds and cut
into small dices.
Put the oil in a large shallow pan, add the
garlic, parsley, chilli flakes and cook for 2
minutes. Add the tomato and cook for 2 more
minutes.
Pour in the wine, increase the heat and cook
for 2 minutes.
Season with salt and pepper, lower the heat
and lay the sole fillets in the pan.
Cover and cook for 5 minutes.
Serve the fillets with the sauce poured over
them.

The fillets bathed in this tomatoey, garlicky
oil, taste wonderful and are best eaten as
soon as they are ready. Any other white fish
fillets may be used for this dish.

FILLETS OF TROUT WITH KING PRAWNS & MARSALA

filetti di trota con gamberoni al marsala

8 fillets of trout about 100g each
20g butter
4 tablespoons extra virgin olive oil
100ml dry marsala
12 king prawns
1 garlic clove, finely chopped
3 tablespoons parsley, finely chopped
½ lemon
salt & freshly milled black pepper

SERVES 4

Peel the prawns, wash and dry on kitchen
paper. Wash the trout fillets and dry on
kitchen paper.
Cut each fillet in half diagonally.
Place the fillets in a greased ovenproof dish,
pour over the oil, add the prawns, garlic,
2 tablespoons of parsley and season with salt
and pepper.
Cover with foil and place in a pre-heated
oven at 180C / gas mark 4.
After 5 minutes, add the marsala, continue
to cook for a further 10 minutes. Drain the
fillets and prawns from the juices and keep
warm.
Put the juices in a small pan, add the lemon
juice, 1 tablespoon of parsley, and cook for 2
minutes.
If necessary, add more salt and pepper.
Arrange the fillets and prawns on a warm
serving dish, pour over the sauce, sprinkle
over the rest of the parsley.

An elegant way of serving trout, this dish is
ideal for dinner parties.

FILLETS OF WHITE FISH IN A COURGETTE & WINE SAUCE

filleti di pesce bianco con salsa di zucchine e vino bianco

600g any white fish fillets
600g courgettes
1 ripe tomato diced
6 tablespoons extra virgin olive oil
200 ml dry white wine
4 tablespoons fresh parsley, finely chopped
4 garlic cloves, finely chopped
salt & freshly milled black pepper

SERVES 4

Put 3 tablespoons of the oil, 2 garlic cloves,
2 tablespoons of parsley and the tomato in
a greased ovenproof dish and put the fillets
on this. Season with salt and pepper.
Cook in a pre-heated oven at 200C / gas mark 6
for 10 minutes. Add 100ml white wine and cook
for 5 minutes.
Trim the courgettes and cut into thin slices.
Put the remaining oil, garlic and parsley in
a pan, add the courgettes, the rest of the wine,
season with salt and pepper and cook on
medium heat until they are soft.
Keep apart sufficient slices to cover the fish
fillets for decoration.
Blend the rest of the courgettes to a smooth
sauce and spoon onto 4 warm plates.
Place the fillets on top of the sauce and
decorate them with the slices of courgettes,
slightly overlapping them so they resemble
the scales of a fish.
Before serving, pour over the juices in the
dish where the fillets have cooked .

Impress your guests with this striking,
delicate tasting and so easy to do, fish dish.

FISH KEBABS

spiedini di pesce

350g monkfish
350g cod
350g salmon
12 small vine tomatoes
100ml olive oil
2 garlic cloves
1 teaspoon chilli flakes
1 sprig rosemary
100ml dry white wine
salt & freshly milled black pepper

SERVES 4

Mix the oil with chilli flakes, add the garlic cloves, rosemary, salt and pepper.
Cut the fish into bite-size chunks and season with salt and pepper.
Place them in the oil mixture, mix well and leave to marinate for 1 hour.
Thread the fish onto the skewers alternating with the tomatoes.
Place them in a greased ovenproof dish, pour over the marinade and cook for 30 minutes.
Remove the garlic and rosemary.
Arrange the kebabs on a warm serving dish.
Pour the juices that are in the dish where the kebabs have cooked, into a saucepan.
Add the wine, increase the heat, cook for a few minutes and then pour over the kebabs.

Instead of cooking them in the oven, these wonderful kebabs can also be cooked on the barbeque.

FISH STEW

zuppa di pesce

1 kg assorted fish (e.g. monkfish, cod,
haddock)
500g king prawns, peeled
1 onion finely chopped
2 garlic cloves, finely chopped
4 anchovy fillets, finely chopped
400g tinned tomatoes, blended
200ml extra virgin olive oil
200ml dry white wine
2 teaspoons chilli flakes
1 teaspoon saffron powder
2 tablespoons fresh chopped parsley
salt and freshly milled black pepper

SERVES 4- 6

Put the oil in a large pan, add the garlic,
half of the parsley and cook for 2-3 minutes.
Add the onion, cook until soft, then add 2
tablespoons of wine, chilli flakes, anchovies
and cook for 2 minutes.
Season with salt and pepper.
Pour in the tomatoes, saffron powder, the
rest of the wine and cook for 20 minutes on
a low heat.
Cut the fish into bite-size pieces, add to the
pan and cook for 5 minutes, add the prawns
and cook for a further 5 minutes.
Turn off the heat and sprinkle with the rest
of the parsley.
Serve with toasted slices of ciabatta bread
rubbed with garlic.

There are many variations of fish stew.
This version with no bones or shelled fish,
makes it easy to prepare and above all,
easy to eat.

MACKEREL FILLETS GRATINATED

filetti di sgombro gratinati

8 mackerel fillets
200g coarsely grated breadcrumbs
2 garlic cloves, finely chopped
2 tablespoons parsley, finely chopped
2 tablespoons French mustard
extra virgin olive oil
salt & freshly milled black pepper

SERVES 4

Put the breadcrumbs into a bowl, add the
garlic, parsley, salt and pepper, mix well.
Pour in enough oil so that the breadcrumbs
bind together.
Wash and dry the fillets.
Spread each one with a little mustard then
press them into the breadcrumb mixture,
well coating both sides.
Place the fillets in a lightly oiled ovenproof
dish and cook them in a pre-heated oven at
180C / gas mark 4 for about 30 minutes
until golden brown.

Sardine fillets may be used for this dish instead
of the mackerel fillets. Also, olive oil can be
used instead of the mustard.

SALMON STEAKS WITH PRAWNS & COURGETTES IN A BAG

salmone con gamberi e zucchine al cartoccio

4 salmon steaks about 200g each, skinned
200g king prawns, peeled
2 medium courgettes, grated
4 tablespoons extra virgin olive oil
4 garlic cloves,
2 shallots, finely chopped
1 tablespoon parsley, finely chopped
4 tablespoons extra virgin olive oil
100ml dry white wine
salt & freshly milled black pepper
baking paper

SERVES 4

Cut 4 x 35cm squares of baking paper. Put
2 tablespoons of oil in a pan with parsley,
courgettes, 2 finely chopped garlic cloves.
Season with salt and pepper, stir well and
cook for about 5 minutes till soft.
In another pan, put 2 tablespoons of oil, 2
finely chopped garlic cloves, the shallots and
cook for a few minutes till soft.
Add the salmon steaks, cook for 2 minutes
each side. Season with salt and pepper.
Add the prawns to the salmon steaks, stir
well, pour in the wine and cook for 2 minutes.
Put each salmon steak in the centre of each
square of paper, arrange the prawns and
courgettes on top.
Draw 2 opposite sides of the paper over the
fish and fold over twice. Tuck the ends of the
paper under the parcel to seal everything in.
Place the parcels on a baking sheet and bake
for 20 minutes in a pre-heated oven at 200C /
gas mark 6.
When cooked, leave to rest for 2 minutes, then
slide the parcels onto warm serving plates.

SEA BASS, BAKED WITH BLACK OLIVES & WHITE WINE

branzino al forno con olive nere

2 medium sea bass, scaled and gutted
10 black olives, pitted
2 cloves garlic, finely chopped
2 tablespoons parsley, finely chopped
100ml extra virgin olive oil
200ml dry white wine
salt & freshly milled black pepper

SERVES 4

Preheat the oven to 200C / gas mark 6.
Season the sea bass with salt and pepper
and place in a greased ovenproof dish.
Add the oil, garlic, parsley, olives and wine.
Bake for 20 minutes, basting with the juices
as the bass cooks.
When cooked place on a warm serving dish
and spoon over the olives and juices.

Fillets of sea bass may be used instead
of whole sea bass.
Cook them for 10 minutes only.

SEA BREAM BAKED IN A BAG WITH TOMATOES & OLIVES

orata al cartoccio con pomodorini ed olive

4 medium size sea bream
6 tablespoons extra virgin olive oil
200ml dry white wine
2 shallots, finely chopped
2 garlic cloves, finely chopped
2 tablespoons parsley, finely chopped
12 cherry tomatoes, halved
12 black olives, pitted
salt and freshly milled black pepper
parchment paper

SERVES 4

Into a bowl put the oil, white wine, garlic,
parsley, shallots, tomatoes and olives.
Season with salt and pepper.
Mix well and leave to marinate for 1 hour.
Cut the parchment paper into four squares
large enough to enclose the fish.
Brush these with oil, and place the fish onto
the centre of each one.
Using your hands, coat the fish well all over
with the marinade.
Close the paper around the fish, seal each
one by twisting the edges, forming parcels
and carefully slide them onto a baking tray.
Cook in a pre-heated oven at 200C / gas mark 6
for 20 minutes. Remove the bags from the
oven and allow them to rest for 2-3 minutes.
To serve, place an unopened bag on each plate.

A wonderful way of presenting a fish dish
is in a bag.
Sea bass can also be used for this dish.

SWORDFISH SLICES STUFFED WITH OLIVES & HERBS

fettine di pesce spada ripiene di olive ed erbe

8 swordfish slices, thinly cut
100g black olives, pitted
200ml dry white wine
1 garlic clove, finely chopped
4 leaves basil, finely chopped
2 leaves mint, finely chopped
4 tablespoons extra virgin olive oil
salt and freshly milled black pepper

SERVES 4

Put the olives, garlic, basil, mint, and 1
tablespoon of the wine in a food processor
and blend until smooth.
Season with salt and pepper.
Spread this mixture on the swordfish slices,
roll them up and secure with a toothpick.
Cook them in a pan with the oil for about 5
minutes until golden brown.
Season with salt and pepper.
Pour over the wine, cover, and cook for 10
minutes. Arrange them on a warm serving
dish and pour over the sauce.

Fresh tuna slices can also be used for this dish.

SWORDFISH WITH OLIVES & CAPERS

pesce spada con olive e capperi

4 slices swordfish about 200g each
4 garlic cloves, peeled
100g black olives, pitted and sliced
2 tablespoons capers, coarsely chopped
6 tablespoons extra virgin olive oil
1 large lemon
2 tablespoons parsley, finely chopped
salt and freshly milled black pepper

SERVES 4

Season the swordfish slices with salt and
pepper.
Cook on a hot, lightly oiled griddle pan for
5 minutes each side.
Drizzle over 2 tablespoons of oil and cook
for a further 3 minutes.
Remove the slices from the pan and arrange
them on a warm serving dish.
Pour the remaining oil into the pan, add the
garlic, olives, capers, lemon juice and cook
for 3 minutes.
Season with salt and pepper, add the parsley,
stir well and pour over the fish.

Fresh tuna slices can also be used for this dish.

TROUT IN A RED WINE SAUCE

trote al vino rosso

2 trout about 200g each (scaled and gutted)
1 carrot finely chopped
½ onion finely chopped
1 bouquet garni (thyme, parsley and bay leaf)
65g butter
10g plain flour
400ml medium bodied red wine
salt & freshly milled black pepper

SERVES 4

Gently cook the carrot, onion and bouquet
garni in 20g of butter for 5 minutes.
Put this mixture on the bottom of a greased
flameproof dish.
Season the trout with salt and pepper and
lay them on top of the mixture.
Pour over the red wine, cover, and cook on
the stove until the wine starts to boil.
Transfer this to a pre-heated oven, cover and
cook at 200C / gas mark 6 for 15 minutes.
Drain the trout from the pan and keep warm.
Pass the juices through a food mill or sieve.
Melt the remaining butter, add the flour, beat
well and stir this into the juices.
Bring to the boil, stir until the sauce thickens
and pour over the trout.

If preferred, fillets of trout can be used instead
of whole trout.
Cook them for 10 minutes only, in the oven.

WHITE FISH FILLETS & PANCETTA WITH SAFFRON & WINE

filetti di pesce bianco e pancetta allo zafferano

600g any white fish fillets
8 pancetta slices
150g button mushrooms, thinly sliced
100ml dry white wine
1 teaspoon saffron powder
2 tablespoons extra virgin olive oil
salt & freshly milled black pepper

SERVES 4

Wrap the pancetta around each fillet and
cook them in a pan with the oil for about 5
minutes each side, until golden brown.
Remove from the pan and keep warm.
In the same pan, add the mushrooms, salt,
pepper, pour over the wine and cook for 5
minutes.
Add the saffron powder and stir well.
Return the fish to the pan, increase the heat
and cook for 3 minutes.
Arrange the fish on a serving dish and pour
over the sauce.

An elegant and refined tasting dish, this is
ideal for dinner parties.

vegetables

-- *aubergine & mozzarella bake*

-- *braised fennel*

-- *cabbage with olive oil, garlic & rosemary*

-- *courgettes, grilled, with roasted red pepper salsa*

-- *french runner beans with garlic & fresh tomato*

-- *mixed vegetable salsa*

-- *peppers, courgettes, tomatoes with ricotta & herbs*

-- *potatoes pizzaiola*

-- *red & yellow peppers with onions & tomatoes*

-- *spinach with garlic, extra virgin olive oil & parmesan*

-- *stuffed aubergines*

-- *yellow peppers baked with fresh tomato & oregano*

AUBERGINE & MOZZARELLA BAKE

melanzane alla parmigiana

400g tinned tomatoes, blended
1 onion, finely chopped
2 cloves garlic, finely chopped
6 tablespoons extra virgin olive oil
4 leaves fresh basil
2 large firm aubergines
2 mozzarellas, sliced
150g grated parmesan cheese
cooking oil for frying
salt and freshly milled black pepper

SERVES 4

Cook the onion and the garlic in the extra
virgin olive oil on a low heat until soft.
Do not let it brown, if necessary add a very
small quantity of water.
Add the tomatoes, basil, season with salt
and pepper and cook for about 30 minutes,
until the sauce has a thick consistency.
Cut the aubergines into slices about 1cm
thick and fry them, in just enough cooking
oil to cover the bottom of a frying pan, a few
minutes each side, till golden brown.
Lay them on kitchen paper to absorb any
excess oil.
Start layering; lightly cover the bottom of an
oiled ovenproof dish with the tomato sauce
and arrange the aubergine slices on top.
Spoon over enough tomato sauce to cover the
slices and place the mozzarella slices on top.
Sprinkle over the parmesan cheese.
Continue to layer in this way finishing with
the mozzarella and parmesan.
Bake in a pre-heated oven at 200C / gas mark
6 for about 40 minutes till golden brown.

BRAISED FENNEL

finocchi gratinati

1 kg fennel
6 tablespoons extra virgin olive oil
100ml milk
100g parmesan cheese, grated
salt & freshly milled black pepper

SERVES 4

Cut the green stalks off the fennel, remove
the tough outer leaves and cut the bulbs into
quarters.
Wash well and put them into a pan with the oil,
cover and cook on a gentle heat until soft.
Season with salt and pepper.
Increase the heat and cook until the fennel is
golden brown.
Add the milk, cook for 5 minutes, stir well.
Arrange the fennel in a greased ovenproof
dish and sprinkle the parmesan cheese over
evenly.
Bake in a pre-heated oven at 180C / gas mark
4 for about 15-20 minutes till golden brown.

Fennel cooked this way has a wonderful flavour
and goes well with fish dishes.

CABBAGE WITH OLIVE OIL, GARLIC & ROSEMARY

cavolo con olio, aglio e rosmarino

1 cabbage
4 garlic cloves
4 sprigs rosemary
8 tablespoons extra virgin olive oil
salt & freshly milled black pepper

SERVES 4

Chop the cabbage roughly, wash thoroughly and put it into a saucepan of cold salted water.
Bring to the boil and cook until very tender. Drain well and try to get as much water out of it as possible.
Put the oil into a pan with the garlic cloves and the rosemary. Cook for 2-3 minutes and then add the cabbage. Stir well.
Season with salt and lots of pepper, cover and cook for ten minutes.
Remove the rosemary before serving.

Just by adding oil, garlic and rosemary, it is surprising how wonderful even boiled cabbage can taste.

COURGETTES, GRILLED, WITH ROASTED RED PEPPER SALSA

zucchine, grigliate, con salsa al peperone rosso

500g courgettes
30g roasted red pepper
2 garlic cloves
2 anchovy fillets
1 lemon
60g extra virgin olive oil
1 tablespoon parsley, finely chopped
salt and freshly milled black pepper

SERVES 4

Trim and slice the courgettes lengthways.
Season with salt and pepper, brush with a
little oil and cook them on a hot griddle pan
until soft.
Arrange them on a serving dish and leave to
cool.
Put the pepper, garlic, anchovies, the juice
of the lemon, parsley and remaining oil, into
a food processor and blend until smooth.
Season with salt and pepper.
Spoon the salsa over the courgettes, mix well
and leave to marinate for 1 hour.

These courgettes, after they have cooked and
marinated, are ideal if cooked on the barbeque
for a few minutes.

FRENCH RUNNER BEANS WITH GARLIC & FRESH TOMATO

fagiolini con aglio e pomodoro fresco

500g French runner beans
3 tablespoons extra virgin olive oil
3 garlic cloves
1 large ripe tomato
salt & freshly milled black pepper

SERVES 4

Put the beans in a saucepan of cold salted water, bring to the boil and cook for 5 minutes.
Drain and place them in a bowl of cold water for 5 minutes. Drain them again and put them into a pan with the oil and the garlic cloves, cut in half.
Chop the tomato into dices, after taking out the seeds and add them to the beans.
Stir well, season with salt and pepper, add a ladle of the water they have cooked in, cover and cook on a low heat for about 15 minutes, until tender.

French beans cooked this way have a fantastic taste.

MIXED VEGETABLE SALSA

Salsa

2 aubergines, cut into dices
4 courgettes, sliced
2 red peppers, sliced
2 green peppers, sliced
2 yellow peppers, sliced
2 onions, sliced
2 carrots, sliced
4 cloves garlic, finely chopped
6 basil leaves
100ml olive oil
400g tinned tomatoes, blended
salt & freshly milled black pepper

SERVES 4

Into a large saucepan put the olive oil,
garlic, aubergines, courgettes, peppers,
onions, carrots, tomatoes, and basil leaves.
Season with salt & pepper.
Cover and cook on a low heat for about 2
hours, stirring occasionally.
The salsa is ready when all the vegetables
are very soft and have blended together.
If there is too much liquid, uncover and cook
for 15 minutes.

This dish may look like a mushy mess but the
flavours of all the vegetables that blend together
are absolutely wonderful. Ideal served with meat,
poultry or fish, it is great on its own with crusty
bread. It is best eaten the day after preparation.

PEPPERS, COURGETTES, TOMATOES WITH RICOTTA & HERBS.

peperoni, zucchine e pomodori con ricotta ed erbe

2 medium size courgettes
4 small red peppers
2 medium size ripe tomatoes
200g ricotta
1 egg
1 teaspoon parsley, finely chopped
1 teaspoon mint, finely chopped
2 tablespoons grated parmesan cheese
1 tablespoon breadcrumbs
2 tablespoons extra virgin olive oil
salt & freshly milled black pepper

SERVES 4

Heat the oven to 200C / gas mark 6.
Put the courgettes and peppers into boiling
water and cook them for 3 minutes.
Cut the tomatoes in half, after taking out
the seeds and then put them, upside down
on kitchen paper, to eliminate the inner
liquid.
Cut the top off the peppers and remove the
seeds and any white membrane.
Cut the courgettes in half, carefully remove
the pulp with a teaspoon, chop it up and put
to one side.
Place these vegetables in an oiled ovenproof
dish and season with salt and pepper.
Prepare the stuffing by mixing, in a bowl, the
ricotta, egg yolk, parmesan cheese, pulp of
the courgette, herbs and breadcrumbs.
Season with salt and pepper.
Whisk the egg white until firm, gently mix it
into the stuffing and spoon this into the
vegetables.
Drizzle with the oil and bake in the oven for
about 30 minutes until the topping is crispy
and golden.

POTATOES PIZZAIOLA

patate alla pizzaiola

750g waxy potatoes, boiled in their skins
400g tinned tomatoes, blended
2 garlic cloves, finely chopped
1 onion, finely chopped
4 tablespoons extra virgin olive oil
2 tablespoons parsley, finely chopped
1 tablespoon dried oregano
salt & freshly milled black pepper

SERVES 4

Start by preparing the tomato sauce; put the
oil in a wide pan, add the onion, half of the
garlic and cook on a gentle heat until soft.
Add the tomatoes, season with salt, pepper,
cover and cook on a low heat for 30 minutes.
Add the rest of the garlic, oregano and the
parsley to the sauce, stir well and cook for
5 minutes.
Peel the potatoes and carefully cut them into
slices about ½cm thick.
Arrange them on the sauce, cover and cook
on a low heat for 5 minutes. Turn them over
carefully so that they do not break, cover and
cook for a further 5 minutes.
Season with more black pepper.
Serve hot.

The tomato sauce and oregano give the
potatoes a 'pizza' taste and are delicious.

RED & YELLOW PEPPERS WITH ONIONS & TOMATOES

Peperonata

2 large red peppers
2 large yellow peppers
400g tinned tomatoes
6 tablespoons extra virgin olive oil
2 onions
salt & freshly milled black pepper

SERVES 4

*Trim the peppers and slice them after
removing the seeds and white membrane.
Peel the onions and slice them.
Chop the tomatoes coarsely.
Put the oil in a pan, add the peppers, onions
and tomatoes.
Season with salt and pepper, cover and cook
on a low heat for about 30 minutes until the
peppers are tender, stirring occasionally.*

*This colourful dish is ideal hot in the winter
and cold in the summer.*

SPINACH WITH GARLIC, EXTRA VIRGIN OLIVE OIL & PARMESAN

spinaci con olio, aglio e parmigiano

1 kg fresh spinach
2 garlic cloves
4 tablespoons extra virgin olive oil
30g butter
50g parmesan cheese, grated
salt and freshly milled black pepper

SERVES 4

Wash the spinach thoroughly and put it into
a high pan without water.
Add a pinch of salt, cover the pan and cook
on a medium heat.
As soon as they start to lower, turn them over
and cook for 1 minute.
In all this should take 3-4 minutes.
Remove from the pan with a slotted spoon.
When cool, squeeze well, with your hands to
remove any excess liquid, chop up roughly.
In a frying pan, heat the oil and butter, add
the garlic cloves cut in half, cook until golden
brown, then remove from the pan.
Put the spinach in the pan, season with salt
and pepper and stir well.
Turn off the heat and sprinkle over the
parmesan.

To make this dish a little creamier, add
4 tablespoons of single cream and stir well,
cook for 2 minutes before turning off the heat
and sprinkling over the parmesan.

STUFFED AUBERGINES

melanzane ripiene

4 medium size aubergines
250g cherry tomatoes
2 garlic cloves, finely chopped
4 tablespoons extra virgin olive oil
1 tablespoon parsley, finely chopped
1 tablespoon basil, finely chopped
1 tablespoon capers, finely chopped
1 tablespoon dried oregano
1 teaspoon chilli flakes
4 tablespoons parmesan cheese, grated
4 tablespoons breadcrumbs, coarsely grated
salt & freshly milled black pepper
vegetable oil

SERVES 4

Trim and wash the aubergines and cut them in half lengthways. Carefully remove the pulp, leaving about 1cm all around, chop it up and keep to one side.
Gently fry the aubergines on both sides, with just enough cooking oil to cover the bottom of a frying pan, until golden brown and slightly soft. Lay them on kitchen paper to absorb any excess oil.
Chop up the tomatoes, after removing the seeds, and put them into a pan with garlic, parsley, capers, basil, chilli flakes and 3 tablespoons of extra virgin olive oil.
Stir well and cook for 5 minutes.
Add the pulp of the aubergines, season with salt and pepper and cook for 10 minutes.
Stir in the breadcrumbs and parmesan, mix well and fill the aubergines with this mixture.
Place them in a greased oven-proof dish.
Sprinkle oregano on top, drizzle with olive oil, bake in a pre-heated oven at 200 C / gas mark 6 for about 30 minutes until golden brown.

YELLOW PEPPERS BAKED WITH FRESH TOMATO & OREGANO

peperoni gialli al forno con pomodoro fresco e origano

4 large yellow peppers
4 large ripe tomatoes
6 tablespoons extra virgin olive oil
1 tablespoon dried oregano
salt & freshly milled black pepper

SERVES 4

Cut the peppers into large pieces and place
in an oiled ovenproof dish, skin side up.
Cut the tomatoes into slices and put a slice
on top of each piece of pepper.
Pour over the olive oil, season with salt and
pepper, sprinkle over the oregano.
Bake in a pre-heated oven at 180C / gas mark
4 for about 30 minutes until the peppers are
tender.

It is amazing how good these peppers taste
considering the very few ingredients used.

desserts

-- *coffee mousse with cream & chocolate sauce*

-- *iced marsala creams with toasted almonds*

-- *lemon & limoncello mousse with strawberry sauce*

-- *orange & mascarpone cheesecakes with orange sauce*

-- *Oriana's tiramisu`*

-- *panettone with mascarpone & meringues*

-- *panna cotta & raspberry sundae*

-- *peach & amaretti biscuit delight*

-- *pears in red wine with mascarpone & marsala sauce*

-- *strawberry delight*

-- *stuffed peaches*

-- *tiramisu`*

COFFEE MOUSSE WITH CREAM & CHOCOLATE SAUCE

mousse al caffe` con crema di cioccolato e panna

200ml espresso coffee
200g whipping cream
4 tablespoons sugar
2 sheets leaf gelatine
50g plain chocolate
50g single cream

SERVES 4

While preparing the coffee, put the gelatine
to soak in a little cold water for 5 minutes
until soft. Drain and squeeze out any excess
liquid.
Pour the hot coffee into a bowl, add the
sugar and stir until it dissolves.
Add the gelatine sheets and stir till they
have completely dissolved. Leave to cool.
Whisk the whipping cream until firm.
Pour the cold coffee into the cream a little
at a time, stirring gently.
Spoon this into 4 tall sundae glasses and
place in the fridge to set, for about 4 hours.
Melt the chocolate in a bowl over hot water
and stir in the single cream, mix well.
Leave to cool.
Before serving, remove the sundae glasses
from the fridge and spoon the chocolate
and cream sauce over the mousse in each
glass.

White chocolate can be used for the sauce
instead of plain chocolate.

ICED MARSALA CREAMS WITH TOASTED ALMONDS

semifreddo al marsala con mandorle tostate

300ml double cream
1 large egg white
4 tablespoons icing sugar
4 tablespoons marsala
50g flaked almonds

SERVES 4

Toast the almonds by putting them on a
baking tray in a moderately warm oven
until they turn golden brown. Leave to cool.
Whisk the cream and when it starts to
thicken, add the sugar and marsala, a little
at a time and whisk again till thick.
Whisk the egg white until stiff and gently
fold this into the cream mixture.
Spoon the mixture into 6 freezer-proof
sundae glasses and freeze for about 3 hours
till firm.
Take them out of the freezer 30 minutes
before serving and sprinkle over the almonds.

These incredibly easy to make creams
make a very delicate dessert.

LEMON & LIMONCELLO MOUSSE WITH STRAWBERRY SAUCE

mousse al limone e limoncello con salsa di fragole

for the mousse
125g fresh lemon juice
50g caster sugar
15g leaf gelatine
4 tablespoons limoncello (lemon liquer)
250g whipping cream
75g egg whites
25g icing sugar

for the sauce
250g fresh strawberries
100g sugar
juice of ½ lemon

SERVES 4

Soak the gelatine in a little cold water for 5 minutes until soft. Drain and squeeze out any excess liquid.
Bring the lemon juice and 50g of sugar to the boil, stir well until the sugar dissolves.
Add the gelatine, stir until it dissolves and leave to cool, add the limoncello.
In a bowl, whip the cream until firm, pour in, a little at a time, the lemon and sugar mix and stir gently.
Whisk the egg whites with the icing sugar until firm, gently add to the cream and lemon mixture.
Pour this into small greased ramekins and put in the fridge for 24 hours.
Before serving, run the tip of a knife around the inside of the ramekins and turn them out onto serving plates that have been sprinkled with icing sugar.
Blend the strawberries with the sugar and lemon until smooth and spoon around the mousse.
Decorate with strawberries and sliced kiwi.

ORANGE & MASCARPONE CHEESECAKES WITH ORANGE SAUCE

tortine di arance e mascarpone con salsa di arance

for the cheesecakes
2 oranges
150g mascarpone
2 tablespoons sugar
8 digestive biscuits crushed
8 amaretti biscuits crushed
50g butter
2 tablespoons unsweetened cocoa powder

for the orange sauce
juice of 2 oranges
rind of 1 orange
100g sugar

SERVES 4

Melt the butter in a pan, add the crushed
biscuits and cook them for 2-3 minutes.
Place 4 greased metal pastry rings onto a
baking tray, spoon the biscuit mixture into
these and press well with the back of a spoon.
Peel 2 oranges, cut the pulp into pieces and
place them in a sieve over a bowl.
When the juices have drained, put the pulp
with 2 tablespoons of sugar and mascarpone
into a food processor and blend until smooth.
Spoon this mixture over the biscuit base in
the rings, cover with cling film and place in
the fridge overnight.
Before serving, make the sauce; put 100g of
sugar in a pan on a gentle heat and when it
starts to caramelise, add the rind of 1 orange,
very finely sliced and continue to cook until it
turns a dark caramel colour. Leave to cool.
Add the juice of 2 oranges and the juices of
the pulp and cook for 5 minutes.
Place the cheesecakes on 4 serving plates
that have been sprinkled with cocoa powder.
Run a knife round the insides of the rings and
lift off. Spoon the sauce over each one.

ORIANA'S TIRAMISU

tiramisu` all'Oriana

150g savoiardi biscuits (sponge fingers)
250ml hot espresso coffee
50g sugar
12 tablespoons marsala wine
250g mascarpone
500g ready made custard
200ml fresh whipping cream
4 tablespoons unsweetened cocoa powder or
50g crushed amaretti biscuits

SERVES 4

Put the coffee and sugar into a bowl, stir
well until the sugar dissolves and add 6
tablespoons of marsala.
Briefly soak the biscuits in this and arrange
them in a serving dish.
Put the mascarpone into a bowl and whisk
lightly, add 6 tablespoons of marsala and
whisk again.
Stir in the custard, a little at a time. Taste,
and if not sweet enough, add more sugar to
suit your taste.
Whip the cream until stiff and gently fold it in
to the mascarpone and custard mixture.
Spoon this over the biscuits evenly, so they
are well covered.
Put in the fridge to cool for 2 hours.
Before serving, dust with the cocoa powder,
sieved, or sprinkle over the crushed amaretti
biscuits.

This version of tiramisu` contains no raw eggs
and is safer, in the summer and for those who
should not eat them.

PANETTONE WITH MASCARPONE & MERINGUES

coppette di panettone, mascarpone e meringa

200g panettone
200g mascarpone
100ml fresh whipping cream
3 tablespoons sugar
4 tablespoons marsala
6 meringues
8 amaretti biscuits crushed

SERVES 4

Cut the panettone into cubes and break up 4
of the meringues into pieces.
Whisk the cream until stiff.
Whisk the mascarpone with the sugar and
marsala and stir in the whisked cream.
Add the panettone and meringues to this
and, gently stir well.
Spoon this mixture into 4 sundae glasses
and leave to cool in the fridge for about 4
hours.
Before serving, remove from the fridge and
sprinkle over the rest of the crushed
meringues and amaretti biscuits.

This delicate dessert is a wonderful way of
using up panettone especially at Christmas.

PANNA COTTA & RASPBERRY SUNDAE

panna cotta con lamponi

400g double cream
100g milk
200g sugar
4 sheets leaf gelatine
300g raspberries
2 tablespoons lemon juice
1 vanilla pod

SERVES 4

Melt 100g of sugar in a pan, add the lemon juice and raspberries and stir gently. Place them in a sieve over a bowl, leave to cool and reserve the syrup.
Soak the gelatine in cold water for 5 minutes until soft, drain and squeeze out any excess liquid.
Split the vanilla pod, scrape out the seeds and add to the cream, milk and 100g sugar in a pan. Simmer gently for 5 minutes, do not let boil.
Remove from the heat, add the gelatine, stir till it completely dissolves and leave to cool slightly.
Divide the raspberries into 4 tall sundae glasses. Pour over the panna cotta and place in the fridge for about 4 hours, until it sets.
Return the raspberry syrup to the pan and cook until it thickens slightly. Leave to cool.
Take the sundaes out of the fridge ten minutes before serving and spoon the syrup over each one.

There is only one word to describe this dessert: sublime

PEACH AND AMARETTI BISCUIT DELIGHT

delizia di pesche e amaretti

4 large, ripe fresh peaches
150g sugar
1 lemon
4 egg yolks
2 tablespoons plain flour
250ml milk
3 slices lemon peel
50g amaretti biscuits, crushed

SERVES 4

Peel the peaches, slice and place them in a
bowl.
Sprinkle with 25g of sugar and pour over
the juice of the lemon.
Leave for 2 hours, stirring occasionally.
Drain the peach slices from the juices and
divide them into 4 tall sundae glasses and
sprinkle over half of the amaretti biscuits.
Put the egg yolks into a saucepan, add 125g
of sugar, mix well, stir in the flour, a little
at a time and beat until smooth.
Slowly pour in the milk and stir well.
Add the lemon peel, cook on a low heat and
bring to the boil, stirring continuously. Turn
off the heat, remove the lemon peel and leave
to cool slightly.
Spoon this over the peaches in the sundae
glasses and place in the fridge to cool for
about 2 hours.
Before serving, spoon over the top of each one,
1 tablespoon of the juices of the peaches and
sprinkle over the remaining amaretti biscuits.

Again, there is only one word to describe this dessert:
sublime.

PEARS IN RED WINE WITH A MASCARPONE & MARSALA SAUCE

pere al vino rosso con crema di mascarpone e marsala

8 small pears
250g mascarpone cheese
200ml fresh single cream
400ml medium bodied red wine
100ml marsala wine
100ml water
150g sugar
2 cinnamon sticks

SERVES 4

Peel the pears, leaving the stalks on and put
them in a saucepan with the red wine, 100g
of sugar, the cinnamon sticks and the water.
Bring to the boil and cook on a gentle heat
for about 30 minutes until tender.
Take the pears out of the pan and continue
to cook the sauce till it thickens slightly, to
a syrup.
Whisk together the mascarpone and cream,
add 50g of sugar and the marsala, a little
at a time and whisk again until smooth.
Spoon the mascarpone cream onto 4 plates
that have been sprinkled with icing sugar.
Cut the pears into fan shapes and place 2
on each plate, on top of the cream.
Spoon little drops of the red wine sauce onto
the cream mixture in each plate and a little
on the pears, just enough to coat them.

The pears can be cooked in advance but
place them onto the cream with the wine
sauce on the serving plates, just before serving.

STRAWBERRY DELIGHT

delizia alle fragole

250g strawberries
225g sugar
4 egg yolks
2 tablespoons flour
250ml milk

SERVES 4

Melt 100g of sugar in a pan, add the strawberries and cook them for 2 minutes. Drain them over a bowl, reserving the syrup. Divide the strawberries into 4 tall sundae glasses.
Put the egg yolks into a saucepan, add 125g of sugar, beat well, stir in the flour and mix well.
Pour in the milk, a little at a time, stirring to avoid any lumps. Bring slowly to the boil on a gentle heat, until it thickens, stirring all the time.
Leave to cool slightly and then spoon this over the strawberries in the sundae glasses. Place them in the fridge to cool for about 2 hours.
Return the syrup to the pan and cook until it thickens slightly. Leave to cool.
Take the strawberry delights out of the fridge ten minutes before serving and spoon the syrup on top of each one.

The name says it all!!

STUFFED PEACHES

pesche ripiene

4 large yellow peaches
50g sugar
30g butter
8 amaretti biscuits, crushed
1 egg yolk
2 tablespoons marsala
50g chopped almonds
1 teaspoon grated lemon rind
1 tablespoon unsweetened cocoa powder
100ml dry white wine

SERVES 4

Cut the peaches in half, take out the stone,
spoon out some of the flesh and put this into
a bowl.
Add the amaretti biscuits, sugar, egg yolk,
almonds, marsala, lemon rind, cocoa powder
and mix well.
Fill the peach halves with this mixture.
Arrange them in a greased ovenproof dish
and sprinkle over the wine.
Put a little butter on each one and bake in
a pre-heated oven at 180 C / gas mark 4 for
about 30 minutes until golden brown.

These peaches, when cooked, can be frozen.
When needed, thaw them out and before serving,
heat them in the microwave.

TIRAMISU`

tiramisu`

4 eggs
100g sugar + 4 tablespoons
500g mascarpone
6 tablespoons marsala wine
250ml hot espresso coffee
150g savoiardi biscuits (sponge fingers)
4 tablespoons unsweetened cocoa powder

SERVES 4

Beat the egg yolks and 100g of sugar with
an electric whisk, until pale and stiff.
Add the mascarpone and whisk again until
smooth, pour in the marsala a little at a
time and whisk again.
In a clean bowl, whisk the egg whites with 2
tablespoons of sugar until stiff. Fold this
into the mascarpone mixture.
Put the coffee into a bowl, add 2 tablespoons
of sugar, stir well so the sugar dissolves, and
briefly soak the savoiardi biscuits in it.
Assemble them in a serving dish.
Spoon over the mascarpone mixture evenly
so the biscuits are well covered, place in the
fridge for 2 hours.
Remove from the fridge 10 minutes before
serving and sprinkle over the sieved cocoa
powder.

For people who do not like liqueur or for children,
do not use the marsala.

INDEX

Published by INGANI PUBLISHERS
September 2004

Printed by AUSTIN ROSE PETERBOROUGH

First Edition

© *A MODO MIO 2004*

ISBN 0 9548675 0 5

Photographs:-

On front cover :
A fan of tomato and buffalo mozzarella

On page 3:
Bresaola with rocket & shavings of parmesan

On back cover in clockwise direction:
Chicken, roasted peppers & olive salad
Pasta with a prawn & asparagus sauce
Orange & mascarpone cheesecake with orange sauce
Fillets of white fish in a courgette & wine sauce